The Elijah message for the

# PROPHETS OF FIRE

# Brian D. Jones

**Pacific Press® Publishing Association**
Nampa, Idaho
Oshawa, Ontario, Canada

Edited by Kenneth R. Wade
Designed by Dennis Ferree
Cover photo/art by Tony Stone Images

Copyright ©1999 by
Pacific Press® Publishing Association
Printed in the United States of America
All Rights Reserved

All Bible texts are quoted from the New King James Version unless otherwise noted.
The author is responsible for the accuracy of all quoted material.

Jones, Brian, 1948-
    Prophets of fire ; the Elijah message for the end time / Brian D. Jones.
        p.   cm.
    Includes bibliographical references.
    ISBN 0-8163-1704-6  (alk. paper)
    1. Elijah (Biblical prophet) 2. John, the Baptist, Saint.
3. Bible—Prophecies—End of the world. I. Title.
BS580.E4J65  1999
222' .5092—dc21                                              98-31887
                                                                CIP

99 00 01 02 03 • 5 4 3 2 1

# Contents

# Introduction

"Behold, I will send you Elijah the prophet before the coming of the great and dreadful day of the Lord. And he will turn the hearts of the fathers to the children, and the hearts of the children to their fathers, lest I come and strike the earth with a curse" (Mal. 4:5, 6). Suspenseful, authoritative, and arresting, these are God's last prophetic words to Israel until the rise of John the Baptist four centuries later. Majestically closing the Old Testament while pointing to the New, this announcement is a warning and promise combined. Christ made clear that one phase of Malachi's prophecy was fulfilled in John the Baptist. But Malachi's words require a second application to complete the prophecy. They predict Elijah's appearance "before the coming of *the great and dreadful day of the Lord*." Plainly, this denotes the period just prior to Christ's second coming, thus giving the prophecy urgent relevance to our time. The aim of this book is to unveil the full significance of Malachi's prophecy concerning Elijah.

We will look at the concentric relationship between the missions and messages of Elijah the Tishbite, John the Baptist, and God's *last day* "Elijah." By clearly understanding the work of the first two "Elijahs" we shall be better able to appreciate the work of God's last "Elijah," who, as we shall see, represents a movement and a people vitally engaged in God's closing work to save a spiritually lost world.

A variety of highly speculative approaches to the great Elijah theme abound. Private interpretations as varied and colorful as autumn leaves (and as devoid of life) have been scattered abroad by many who fancy themselves to be the ultimate Elijah. Such often wield the prophecy as a weapon against God's organized church. Using His prophetic Word as a lure to call people into offshoot cliques of the quintessentially "sanctified," they exalt themselves as the only faithful ones left in spiritual Israel, the only ones who have not bowed the knee to Baal. As we shall see, this is an abuse—a fruitless, frigidly cloistered interpretation of the message. In no way is the Elijah message designed to breed self-righteous exclusivity. Its true effect is to turn "the hearts of the fathers to the children, and the hearts of the children to the fathers." Rather than a summons to alienation, it is a ringing call to reconciliation—reconciliation to God on His uncompromising terms of truth and love; reconciliation to the fullness of His redeeming purpose for humanity.

Fearing the true exposition of the final Elijah message, Satan has crowded in a host of counterfeit views. If he cannot sidetrack Christians with these spurious interpretations, he hopes to discourage them from looking into the subject at all. Often he succeeds by convincing some that the Elijah message is the specialty of wild fanatics or else too unimportant to warrant notice. But the message is in the Bible; and, as we have seen, it is designated as having *special application to the closing days*. Therefore we should not fear to study it in a reverential, biblically-balanced way, with guidance from the Holy Spirit. This message is too sacred and solemn to be ignored or to be taken over by self-proclaimed prophets building on a foundation of angry egotism.

In common with all the prophetic teachings of Scripture, the Elijah message makes those who rightly receive it humble, compassionate, self-transcending, and courageously loyal to God. It stirs hearts to reform but not to rebellion or to estrangement from God's remnant church. A true grasp of the Elijah message will galvanize and unify the church through the power of God's Spirit of truth working freely to enlighten our minds and uproot every weed of worldliness, error, and sin from our hearts. May the present work contribute to accomplishing this purpose for the glory of God and the benefit of His people.

# CHAPTER

# 1

# Elijah the Tishbite

Reformers. What does the word bring to your mind? Radicals, revolutionaries, incendiaries, fanatics? Or trailblazers for truth, pioneers of progress, champions of justice, defenders of the downtrodden?

In his youth Abraham Lincoln saw the activities at a slave market in New Orleans. Seeing the cruel oppression of a whole race of God's children who differed from their buyers and sellers only in skin color, Lincoln determined to abolish slavery by all lawful means the future might place in his hands. The resolution he formed that day shaped his character and lifework and changed the destiny of his nation. He spearheaded a social and political reformation that kept the United States from declining into an assortment of parasitic fiefdoms dependent for their prosperity on others' servitude.

This world owes much to reformers but rarely acknowledges its debt to them in their day.[1] And when it does, it hardly takes in the full scope of their work and the permanence of their legacy. Still more rarely does it give reformers encouragement in the early days of their mission. Yet all true reformers are in voluntary bondage to a mission—that of liberating the human soul. Such was Elijah, one of the greatest reformers the world has ever known.

Elijah lived in Israel during some of the brightest days of its material prosperity. To worldly minds Israel had never been in better circumstances. Life was good. Crops were abundant, wealth was available to the ambitious, Israel's borders were large and seemingly secure. But Israel dwelt in the midnight of spiritual apostasy. Baal worship, with all its degrading practices, had virtually replaced the worship of the true God. The majority of Israel's populace was inclined to give Baal credit for the nation's prosperity, and enthusiasm for pagan worship was on the rise.

At this time Israel's ten northern tribes, under Ahab's rule, had been a separate power for no more than seventy-five years.[2] During that short period the nation had quickly become paganized. Israel's faithful priests who had escaped martyrdom moved to Jerusalem to serve the Lord there without interference (see 2 Chron. 11:13-17). Jezebel, a licentious heathen princess, ruled Israel through her weak, godless husband, Ahab. She established idolatry on a grand scale in his court, maintaining a large retinue of prophets and priests devoted to Baal, the god of the Phoenicians and Canaanites. Sexual immorality and witchcraft were the main features of Baal worship,[3] the chief object of which was to practice licentiousness in the name of religion. "Feel good about yourself while violating the commandments of God" was the force of Baalism. Satanic warpage of character was the fruit. And that fruit abounded in Israel during Elijah's day.

What could one man do to reverse the tide of such rampant apostasy engulfing the nation? Elijah began where so many great movements have begun—in prayer. Not despairing, dejected prayer, not listless petitions tinged with doubt, but fervent, effectual prayer, motivated by love (see James 5:17). And he did something else besides pray. He also pondered Israel's deep fall from true worship and sought a solution.

> As Elijah saw Israel going deeper and deeper into idolatry, his soul was distressed and his indignation aroused. . . . Viewing this apostasy from his mountain retreat, Elijah was overwhelmed with sorrow. In anguish of soul he besought God to arrest the once-favored people in their wicked course, to visit them with judgments, if need be, that they might be led to see

in its true light their departure from heaven. He longed to see them brought to repentance, before they should go to such lengths in evil-doing as to provoke the Lord to destroy them utterly.[4]

Elijah was not vindictive. He wasn't stirred with animosity toward Israel but with heartbroken love. What could be done to awaken Israel from its sensual sleep and set the nation free from idolatry? When gentle reasoning and persuasion won't change obstinate sinners, sometimes discipline will. The wages of sin is death. Pure justice demands the death of the rebellious, but Elijah was a representative of God's mercy tempering His justice. Therefore he prayed that "it would not rain" (James 5:17). Elijah didn't want to see the people suffer but to recognize life's true Source of blessings. He longed to see them restored to worshiping the Creator, which in turn would restore them to spiritual soundness. He saw that such moral renovation would never be possible while his people continued in idolatry, whose degrading effects they failed to recognize.

Scripture repeatedly states that idolatrous worship pollutes the human soul and ultimately debases it to a level lower than that of beasts. See, for example, Psalms 106:34-39, 115:4-8, Isaiah 44:9-20, and Romans 1:18-32. Why does such extreme degradation result from idolatry? Because those who engage in it are actually worshiping devils, even if unwittingly. The Lord said to Israel that when His people in their prosperity forsook worshiping Him, the provider of all blessings, and turned to heathen rites through the influence of surrounding nations, they "sacrificed to demons, not to God" (Deut. 32:17).

In his typically forthright way, Paul deals with this same subject in the context of Christian versus pagan worship: "What am I saying then? That an idol is anything, or what is offered to idols is anything? But I say that the things which the Gentiles sacrifice they sacrifice to demons and not to God, and I do not want you to have fellowship with demons" (1 Cor. 10:19-21).

No wonder the Israelites' moral behavior grew progressively worse as they plunged deeper and deeper into heathen worship! They were worshiping devils, even if they thought themselves too sophisticated to believe in them. One does not have to believe in the existence of one's enemy in order to come under his control. In fact, it puts Satan on vantage ground if people do not believe in him. Then he can go about his nefarious work with less interference, just as a burglar can steal more if no one believes he exists, not suspecting his presence or pilferage.

In America today, outright heathen worship is relatively rare. But this does not mean that idolatry, or devil-worship, is becoming extinct.

> The present age is one of idolatry, as verily as was that in which Elijah lived. No outward shrine may be visible; there may be no image for the eye to rest upon; yet thousands are following after the gods of this world—after riches, fame, pleasure, and the pleasing fables that permit man to follow the inclinations of the unregenerate heart. Multitudes have a wrong conception of God and His attributes, and are as truly serving a false God as were the worshipers of Baal. Many even of those who claim to be Christians have allied themselves with influences that are unalterably opposed to God and His truth. Thus they are led to turn away from the divine and to exalt the human. . . .
>
> Human theories are exalted and placed where God and His law should be. . . . There is seen a spirit of opposition to the plain word of God, of idolatrous exaltation of human wisdom above divine revelation. . . . A faith such as actuated Paul, Peter, and John, they regard as old-fashioned, mystical, and unworthy of the intelligence of modern thinkers.[5]

And yet it was the old-fashioned faith of the apostles that opened the way for the blessing of Pentecost. It is that same old-fashioned faith that will open the way for God's remnant to receive the latter rain, God's final outpouring of the Holy Spirit.

But to return to Elijah's challenge; he prayed that it might not rain until the people came to their senses spiritually. Here Elijah appealed to God on the legal basis of His promise and warning to

Israel, uttered through Moses centuries before: " 'And it shall be that if you earnestly obey My commandments which I command you today, to love the Lord your God and serve Him with all your heart and with all your soul, then I will give you the rain for your land in its season, the early rain and the latter rain, that you may gather in your grain, your new wine, and your oil. And I will send grass in your fields for your livestock, that you may eat and be filled.' Take heed to yourselves, lest your heart be deceived, and you turn aside and serve other gods and worship them, lest the Lord's anger be aroused against you, and He shut up the heavens so that there be no rain, and the land yield no produce, and you perish quickly from the good land which the Lord is giving you" (Deut. 11:13-17).

We can see that Elijah did not arbitrarily choose the form of discipline that he asked God to employ. He prayed in harmony with God's Word, asking only that, since all milder measures had failed, His threatened punishments now be strenuously applied until they accomplished their purpose—to humble Israel's rebellious spirit and bring them to a repentance that would free them from Satan's control and turn their hearts to the true God.

This was a warning judgment, not a final casting off. It was sent in mercy, not in enmity to God's people. How often has God had to deal with your life and mine in similar fashion to awaken us from our carnal trances, our deluded dreams, our rebellious wanderings? "But when we are judged, we are chastened by the Lord, that we may not be condemned with the world" (1 Cor. 11:32).

Consider Manasseh, the worst king Judah ever had. Although the son of Hezekiah, a godly ruler, Manasseh was a renegade. Upon his father's death, he terminated public worship of the true God and imposed the most flagrant forms of heathen worship on his people. As though he were the devil himself, Manasseh destroyed all the true prophets he could find. Merciless, cold, greedy, and oppressive, not a spark of decency flickered in Manasseh's heart. His throne was a stronghold of destruction and death, a seat of evil as cruel as any ever occupied by a tyrant. God sent the king of Assyria to punish Manasseh, who was led in chains to Nineveh, there to molder in a dungeon without hope of pardon or reprieve.

In this prison Manasseh came to his senses and truly repented of his desperate wickedness. His was no calculated "jailhouse conversion." It was true, sincere, and deep. Before he was afflicted Manasseh went astray, but under the rod of divine discipline he genuinely repented. Prison did not convert him, the Lord did; but He had to surround Manasseh with grim walls of stone before He could penetrate his stony heart. Manasseh fell repentantly on the Rock Jesus and was broken. Then the Lord moved on the heart of the Assyrian king to free Manasseh and restore him to his throne in Judah.

Broken and feeble, Manasseh did his best to repair the damage he had inflicted on his nation. Although his credibility was wrecked in the eyes of his people, he was redeemed in the eyes of God and died a saved man. This story is told in 2 Chronicles 33. Read it, and you will never again underestimate the power of God's patience, mercy, and saving grace, which are often most effectively applied in His sternest acts of discipline.

## Questions for Discussion and Reflection

1. Why are reformers generally feared and misunderstood?

2. Why was Elijah distressed about Israel's apostasy?

3. Why did he pray that it would not rain?

4. In what way are God's warning judgments really acts of mercy?

---

1. Henry Ward Beecher wrote: "No man can accomplish that which benefits the ages and not suffer. Discoverers do not reap the fruits of what they discover. Reformers are pelted and beaten. Men who think in advance of their times are persecuted. They who lead the flock must fight the wolf." Quoted in *Mountain Trailways For Youth*, by Mrs. Charles E. Cowman (Los Angeles: Cowman Publications, 1956), 100.

2. In 931 B.C. Jeroboam I led the ten northern tribes of Israel into secession from the tyrannical reign of Solomon's son, Rehoboam, leaving him only with Judah and Benjamin. God gave the northern kingdom to Jeroboam with the stipulation that he should rule it in accordance with divine law. Jeroboam failed to do this and quickly led Israel

into the depths of apostasy (see 1 Kings 11–13). One bad ruler after another forwarded the renegade nation in its downward path. Ahab (874–853 B.C.), Israel's sixth ruler from Jeroboam, dragged his nation into previously unparalleled depths of heathenism. It would seem from the events recorded in 1 Kings 16:29–22:40 that Elijah arose in the early to middle portion of Ahab's twenty-two-year reign.

3. I do not wish to dwell on the hideous pollutions of Baal worship, but the following description of its character is helpful in ascertaining why Baalism was so strongly condemned in God's Word. "Half Sun-god, and half Bacchus [the god of wine and revelry] ... Baal was worshipped under the image of a bull, 'the symbol of the male power of generation.' In the wantonness of his rites he was kin to Peor; in their cruel atrocity to the kindred Moloch; in the demand for victims to be sacrificed to the horrible consecration of lust and blood he resembled the Minotaur, the wallowing 'infamy of Crete,' with its yearly tribute of youths and maidens. What the combined worship of Baal and Asherah was like (and by Jezebel and Ahab's connivance they were now countenanced in Samaria—we may learn from the description of their temple at Apheka. It confirms what we are incidentally told of Jezebel's devotions. It abounded in wealthy gifts, and its multitude of priests, women, and mutilated ministers . . . were clad in splendid vestments. Children were sacrificed by being put in a leather bag and flung down from the top of the temple, with the shocking expression that 'they were calves, not children.' In the forecourt stood two gigantic phalli. The *Galli* [eunuch priests], maddened into a tumult of excitement by the uproar of drums, shrill pipes, and clanging cymbals, gashed themselves with knives and potsherds, and often ran through the city in women's dress. Such was the new worship with which the dark murderess insulted the faith in Jehovah. Could any condemnation be too stern for the folly and faithlessness of the king who sanctioned it?" Frederick. W. Farrar, D.D., *The First Book of Kings*, second edition (London: Hodder and Stoughton, 1904), 352, 353.

4. *Prophets and Kings*, 119, 120.

5. Ibid., 177, 178.

# CHAPTER

# 2

# Elijah Confronts Israel's Apostasy

God commissioned Elijah to go before the king and pronounce His judgment against Israel, an errand that took exceptional courage. It's hard to confront perversely wicked people, especially if they are in high places. Their cold frown and reckless abuse of power silences many a dissenting voice. How often do good people say nothing in protest against evil because they fear offending those in power.

But Elijah's faith and love overrode his fears. He had a divine commission to speak and ran not in his own authority. As we have seen, long before he spoke God's sentence of judgment in Ahab's court, Elijah had poured out earnest prayers of intercession for Israel. Every fiber of his being was bound up with the interests of God's erring nation. Elijah hated sin but had no animosity toward the sinful; he longed for their salvation and for Israel's restoration. Many would-be Elijah's today need to remember this.

It is easy for some people of aggressive temperament to denounce sin and apostasy in others, while their own hearts are in the strangling grip of anger, pride, or some other evil passion. Bursting with indignation and harsh words, they have only the dimmest sense of God's love and restorative purpose even in His most severe discipline. They run with their message of wrathful doom but are not sent by the God of Israel.[11]

But Elijah "did not seek to be the Lord's messenger; the word of the Lord came to him. And jealous for the honor of God's cause, he did not hesitate to obey the divine summons, though to obey seemed to invite swift destruction at the hand of the king."[22]

What was Elijah's burden? What did he see that most of his contemporaries missed? Two things: the extreme sinfulness of sin and the surpassing glory of Christ's righteousness. Which Israelite of Elijah's day would not readily have admitted to being a sinner? Which would not have acknowledged that God was righteous—infinitely so.

In terms of declared belief, Israel seemed strongly religious. True, their religion was polluted with idolatry, but this doesn't mean the average worshiper would have said that immorality was acceptable. They believed in Jehovah, they believed that Baal and the gods all stood for basic decency. But real spirituality was rare. While the form of godliness abounded, the power of godly living was woefully absent. The world and its ways took center stage—then, as now.

Elijah saw the falsity of his people's religious views and attitudes. He recognized that religion had become a vehicle for self-display, self-worship, and self-merit. God was simply a personage created in the likeness of the worshipers. For most people the idea of obedience to divine law seemed strangely remote, antiquated, unrealistic, dispensable. Fine for ascetics and legalists but irrelevant for progressive people living in the "real" world.

Elijah also saw that drought and famine were far less devastating woes than unchecked rebellion against God. Appeals and remonstrances from Israel's earlier prophets had brought about no change for the better. God could have abandoned His people to their idols and let them reap fully as they had sown. But He loved His erring people; He longed to free them from their delusions and bring them back into a healthy relationship with Himself. He wanted their souls to be like a well-watered garden, full of the fruits and flowers of Paradise, instead of the briars of Baaldom. Yet the Israelites saw no advantage to changing. They were prospering in their worldliness and rebellion. Their religion seemed to be a fine ecumenical mixture of the worship of Jehovah and Baal, progressive, contemporary, and thriving. What need to repent and return to the old ways?

Israel's obstinacy compelled God to resort to "tough love." It was His desperate warning to a people who were cavorting with devils on a festive jaunt into the abyss. He would withhold rain until they discovered how parched their souls had become even in the days of their most sparkling pleasures and luxurious prosperity. Elijah was no cynic; he did not see Israel's situation as hopeless. "He fully believed that God would humble His apostate people and that through the visitation of His judgments He would bring them to humiliation and repentance. He ventured everything in the mission before him."[33]

So without prelude or apology Elijah strode into the presence of King Ahab. What revel or debauch he interrupted by this appearance we can only guess. But Elijah came clothed in heaven's armor and in the thunder of God's power. He spoke the sentence of the Supreme Potentate, "As the Lord God of Israel lives, before whom I stand, there shall not be dew nor rain these years, except at my word" (1 Kings 17:1). King, courtiers, and palace guards were alike stunned and transfixed. None dared make a move toward Elijah; the Lord was his shield and buckler. As abruptly as he came, Elijah left, leaving the palace to its reflections on Israel's much-deserved but long-delayed punishment.

*Questions for Discussion and Reflection*

1. What do the following texts in Hosea reveal about Israel's spiritual condition around the time of Elijah? Hos. 1:2; 2:7-10, 13; 11:7.

2. What do the following texts reveal about God's love for His people? Hos. 2:14-20; 11:8, 9; 14:4-8.

3. Describe a situation in your life in which you needed the chastisement of God. What do you think would have happened to you if the Lord had let you go on uncorrected? See 2 Chron. 33:9-13; Ps. 119:67, 71; Rev. 3:19.

4. "The work of apostasy begins in some secret rebellion of the heart against the requirements of God's law. Unholy desires, un-

lawful ambitions are cherished and indulged, and unbelief and darkness separate the soul from God." (*That I May Know Him*, 254). What insight does this statement give you into the challenge that God faced in His efforts to bring Israel back to a right relationship with Himself? What insight does it give you into the challenges Elijah faced?

---

1. We must be careful, however, not to run to the opposite extreme of supposing that every word of reproof and warning is unchristian or satanically inspired. Ellen White wrote, "Somebody is to come in the spirit and power of Elijah, and when he appears, men may say, 'You are too earnest, you do not interpret the Scriptures in the proper way. Let me tell you how to teach your message' " (*Selected Messages*, 1:412).
But God's true servants, though they must warn and reprove His erring people, do not turn against the church like ravening wolves, denouncing its leadership and calling people out of the fellowship of the church into their own small offshoot groups, each vying to be recognized as God's premier representative. We have innumerable warnings against this breed of self-styled prophets. See, for example, Prov. 18:1; 1 Cor. 1:10, 13; 11:19; 1 John 2:19; *Testimonies to Ministers*, 61, 488. They may be ever so sincere, but they are deeply misled. Without realizing it, they obscure and hinder the work of those whom the Lord commissions to speak to His people in the spirit and power of Elijah. A disposition to assault the church or the apostate powers of the world is no proof of sanctity. "Some who are now ready to take up weapons of warfare will in times of real peril make it manifest that they have not built upon the solid rock; they will yield to temptation. Those who have had great light and precious privileges, but have not improved them, will, under one pretext or another, *go out from us*"—(*Maranatha*, 202 [emphasis supplied]; see also *Maranatha*, 157). God chooses as spokespersons those who are self-transcendingly loyal to the truth *and* to the church.

2. *Prophets and Kings*, 120, 121.

3. *Testimonies for the Church*, 3:275. See also *Maranatha*, 69, which magnificently describes how sinners can come back to God through the repentance that He seeks to kindle in every heart. When any make this transaction with God, "a sweet heavenly peace will pervade the mind, and you will love to meditate upon God and heaven. You will feast upon the glorious promises of His word. . . ." (*Maranatha*, 69).

# CHAPTER
# 3

# Elijah's Prophecy Fulfilled

**D**eparting as suddenly as he came, Elijah left behind him a stunned, electrified court. Once recovered from its initial shock, however, it became a hornets' nest of activity. Courtiers and king bristled with fury. Guards fanned out all over the countryside to arrest the intruder. But God swiftly placed Elijah beyond their reach.

It had taken strong faith and courage for Elijah to bear so weighty a message. On the way from his country retreat to the king's palace in Samaria, Elijah saw thick forests and green hillsides, laced with abundantly flowing brooks and streams. No visible evidence suggested that soon these countless watercourses would dry up; that fields, valleys, and forests would turn yellow from drought. But Elijah gave no place to unbelief. Having a mandate from God, he carried it out briskly and decisively.

Elijah's earthly life would never again be uneventful or free from conflict. He had a mission to complete, and the nation he was sent to help had little appreciation for his task. In fact, they wished he had never gotten started. Opposition to God's messengers is not rare. Paul wrote the searching question to the Christians in Galatia, "Have I now become your enemy by telling you the truth?" (Gal. 4:16, TEV). To the Corinthians he wrote, "And I will very gladly spend and be spent for your souls; though the more abundantly I love you, the less I am loved" (2 Cor. 12:15). And David plaintively penned, "I am for peace: but when I speak, they are for war" (Ps. 120:7).

Because of his love for God and Israel, Elijah's "whole life was devoted to the work of reform."[11] But Satan didn't want reformation for Israel, and Israel didn't want it for themselves. Knowing the immediate peril His prophet would face for his valiant performance of duty, God told Elijah, "Get away from here and turn eastward, and hide by the Brook Cherith, which flows into the Jordan. And it will be that you shall drink from the brook, and I have commanded the ravens to feed you there" (1 Kings 17:3, 4).

Meanwhile, as Ahab's spies combed the land in their fruitless manhunt, they gave unintended prominence to Elijah's message. From lip to lip flew the question, "What did Elijah do, what did he say, that so enraged the king's court?" Thus his prophecy found wide circulation. God thereby harnessed the rebellious fury of man to bring glory to Himself (see Ps. 76:8-10). God's faithful few must have quietly rejoiced that apostasy had finally been challenged, while most Israelites seethed with resentment that Elijah had interrupted their carnival with Satan.

Neither the king's anger nor the nation's unbelief could stop the prophecy from going into immediate effect. Months went by without a drop of rain. Drought took its increasingly noticeable toll as brooks dried up, fields turned from yellow to brown, while trees withered and shed masses of rattling leaves. Lakes and rivers became bone dry; the air grew hot, suffocating, and dust-laden. Baal and Ashtoreth had opportunity to prove Elijah false, but God had spoken, and these heathen deities had no reality, no power to reverse His word. Baal-worshiping priests kept up the farce of their sacrifices and incantations, appealing to Baal to send rain, while water became more and more scarce. No amount of effort to propitiate the heathen gods brought the least sign of moisture from earth or sky.

Still Israel would not repent or accept the lesson God wished them to learn—that all blessings come from Him, the Creator and Sustainer of the universe. Israel groped for some explanation for the drought other than Elijah's stark prophecy. They turned to denouncing the prophet who had declared judgment against their gods and way of worship. If only he could be found and killed, then their gods would be appeased and their troubles would end. Urged on by wicked Queen Jezebel, Ahab intensified his search for Elijah, while God continued to keep His prophet safe.

Furious for being challenged and baffled, Jezebel determined to have all Jehovah's prophets in Israel slain (see 1 Kings 18:4, 13). She would have accomplished her objective had it not been for the quietly courageous Obadiah, Ahab's chief steward, who hid a hundred prophets in two caves and fed them at the risk of his own life. Obadiah was undoubtedly one who had not bowed the knee to Baal but served the Lord in secret in order to protect God's prophets.

As the drought in Israel extended without relief month after month, terror began to creep into the people's hearts. Especially fearful were the prophets and priests of Baal, many of whom knew that their religion was nothing but a colossal fraud but one that had proven materially profitable until Elijah's interference. To pacify the people's consciences and quell their own fears, these false prophets declared with a confidence they wished were real, "Fear not the God of Elijah, nor tremble at His word."[2] These expressions of bogus comfort negated the understanding that God would have His people cherish in all generations: "The fear of the Lord is the beginning of wisdom." "This is the one I esteem: he who is humble and contrite in spirit, and trembles at my word" (Prov. 9:10; Isa. 66:2, NIV).

And so the nation went on, entrenched in stubborn but increasingly nervous defiance, while they waited for nature to take its course or for Baal to finally get active or maybe for God to do something dramatic, something miraculous and—perhaps (profoundly disturbing.

All the while God patiently waited and withheld the rain, until the people were ready to be aroused from their benumbing superstitions and begin to thirst again for Him. His discipline may have seemed harsh, but He exercised it only as a last desperate remedy. The Lord had sent many prophets before Elijah, who made gracious, earnest appeals to the people, but their kindest entreaties only aroused the nation's rage. They despised the prophets and killed many of them, to silence their inspired counsel. (Read 2 Chron. 36:15, 16; Matt. 21:33-42; *Prophets and Kings*, 108.)

It was not God's purpose to destroy His people but to keep them from destroying themselves through sin. Far better to have three years of drought that would lead to repentance and eternal life than to permit Israel to flourish for a few more decades in sin and lose all prospect of heaven as they drifted farther and farther into evil. So great was God's love for His spiritually vagrant people that some years later, under the ministry of Hosea, He even prepared words of repentance for them to speak when they were ready to come back. "O Israel, return to the Lord your God, for you have stumbled because of your iniquity; take words with you, and return to the Lord. Say to Him, 'Take away all iniquity; receive us graciously, for we will offer the sacrifices of our lips. Assyria shall not save us, we will not ride on horses, nor will we say any more to the work of our hands, "You are our gods." For in You the fatherless find mercy' " (Hos. 14:1-3).

In response to their anticipated words of contrition, the Lord promised: " 'I will heal their waywardness and love them freely, for my anger has turned away from them. I will be like the dew to Israel; he will blossom like a lily. Like a cedar of Lebanon he will send down his roots; his young shoots will grow. His splendor will be like an olive tree, his fragrance like a cedar of Lebanon. Men will dwell again in his shade. He will flourish like the grain. He will blossom like a vine, and his fame will be like the wine from Lebanon. O Ephraim, what more have I to do with idols? I will answer him and care for him. I am like a green pine tree; your fruitfulness comes from me' Who is wise? He will realize these things. Who is discerning? He will understand them. The ways of the Lord are right; the righteous walk in them, but the rebellious stumble in them" (Hos. 14:4-9, NIV).

In my own life I have benefited from God's therapeutic discipline. Christ's love pulled on my heart for several years before I accepted His salvation. Driven by the ambition to be a successful jazz performer, I instinctively recognized the conflict between my sensual music and the spirit of heaven's praise. I wanted to be right with God and attuned to heaven's way, but I also wanted to pursue my passion for jazz. Yet, as I discovered, it was not only hard but impossible to hold these discordant interests together.

Paul declared, "For the cravings of the lower nature are opposed to the Spirit, and the Spirit is opposed to the lower nature, because these are antagonistic to each other" (Gal. 5:17, Weymouth's Translation). This truth became poignantly evident to me in my struggle with debased music. Only after I had been deeply involved with jazz for over a decade did I realize that it was a carnal passion warring against my soul. Pride and prolonged habit made me resist conviction. As I resisted, I became more and more desiccated and dissatisfied within. The more tenaciously I clung to my idol, the more miserable I was. My spiritual life was in drought. Finally, I saw that my idolatrous love for worldly music was neutralizing my attraction to Christ. This led me to pray, hesitantly at first, that if God wanted me to give up jazz altogether, He would help me lose all interest in playing it. Without delay, He answered this prayer. The veil was lifted from my ears, and now I heard jazz with anointed insight into its depraved character. My deep involvement with the sultry, sensuous influences of nightclub music had made me feel an arrogant contempt for the traditional Christian hymns I heard in church, as though they were dull and plodding.

Now I saw how deceived I had been. Satan was infusing me with his own attitude to hymns and spiritual songs as he kept the flame of devotion to jazz alive in my heart, which he meant to maintain as an altar of Baal worship. But once having repudiated jazz both as a player and listener, peace came into my heart. A major obstruction had been removed, freeing me to enjoy the pure strains of Christian music untainted by worldly characteristics. My worship experience came alive, for now nothing stood between my soul and the Savior.[3]

Had the Lord permitted me success as a jazz-performer and left my conscience undisturbed about that form of music, I would probably have been content to go on playing it until my death. Thus I would have rejected the Spirit's influence for the dubious and murky pleasure of reveling in sounds that bewitched myself and others. I thank the Lord for the temporary drought He sent into my life, so

that I would turn my parched soul to God and find all the springs of
my joy to be in Him—forever.

*Questions for Discussion and Reflection:*

1. Identify at least two reasons why Elijah had to have strong
faith to take God's message to Ahab's court.

2. Why do so many people find God's messages of truth unpalat-
able or insulting? How would it affect your character development
if God unconditionally accepted every activity you chose, every
attitude you possessed, every idea you believed? If your friends
and family "loved" you too much to ever point out your sins and
mistakes, how would that affect your ability to have a positive influence in this world? How would it affect your capacity to enjoy
heaven?

3. Have you ever prayed that God would take away your love for
some cherished sin? What resulted from your prayers? Do you
have some cherished sin in your life that you have avoided praying
about? Are you willing now to let God deal with you on that matter? If not, why?

4. How do you perceive God—as One who is perpetually angry
with you for your faults and shortcomings or as One who longingly
desires your salvation and labors kindly to bring you into a right
relationship with Himself? How does your view compare with such
passages as Ezekiel 18:3-32; Hosea 2:14-20; 6:1-3; 11:1-4; Micah
7:7-9, 18-20?

---

1. *Prophets and Kings*, 119.

2. *Prophets and Kings*, 123, 124.

3. Carnal "worship" music is one of the key avenues through which Satan is attacking God's remnant church in these last days. It behooves every church member to
make a careful study of this subject. Those who are promoting jazz-rock idioms in
modern church music, no matter in how muted or disguised a form, little realize
what an assault this is on the integrity of pure worship. Sensual religious music

subverts true revival. For a better understanding of this subject, see the Spring 1998 issue of *Adventists Affirm*, devoted to the study of appropriate music for worship. This issue includes a full reprint of the tract, *Guidelines Toward a Seventh-day Adventist Philosophy of Music*, first published by the General Conference of Seventh-day Adventists, 1972. See also *Selected Messages*, 2:31-37.

# CHAPTER

# 4

# Elijah Among the Gentiles

Elijah's heaven-shielded exile during Israel's drought wasn't a time of extensive public labor for him. However, his activities, though unnoticed by the worldly great, had a far-reaching effect on the Gentile world.

His first phase of flight from Ahab took Elijah to an isolated wilderness. During this time, ravens proved more responsive to God's authority than did His chosen people (see Isa. 1:2, 3; Jer. 8:7). These unclean birds fed Elijah by the brook Cherith for a year. When the brook dried up, God directed His servant to Zarephath of Sidon, a province of Phoenicia. This was Jezebel's native country. Ironically, he found greater welcome and security there than in Israel, an example of the proverb that a prophet is not without honor, except in his own country and among his own kin (Matt. 13:57).

As with most prophets, Elijah's work and message were of universal scope. God sends prophets not just to enlighten some small, privileged sect of humanity but all who will hear His voice through His servants (Isa. 45:22; Jer. 1:5; 18:7-9; Ezek. 39:21-27; Dan. 12:9, 10; Amos 9:11, 12; Mic. 4:1-3). "The eyes of the Lord run to and fro throughout the whole earth, to show his might in behalf of those whose heart is blameless toward him" (2 Chron. 16:9, RSV).

God knew a faithful heathen woman who was far more of an

"Israelite" spiritually than most Jews. Through Elijah He brought her the blessing of salvation that, thus far, the majority of His professed people had scorned. Of humble and receptive heart, she honored God supremely, and as a result was prepared to honor His prophet. Accordingly, God commanded Elijah, "Arise, go to Zarephath, which belongs to Sidon, and dwell there. Behold, I have commanded a widow there to feed you" (1 Kings 17:9, RSV).

Like a scorching fever, famine had stalked the land far beyond Israel's borders on into Sidon. Sidon, like Isreal, was steeped in Baal worship, but this widow was a noble exception. "She was a believer in the true God and had walked in all the light that was shining on her pathway."[1] Jesus pointed out that many widows lived in Israel in the days of Elijah. No less surely many widows lived in Sidon. But Elijah was sent to this particular widow, because of her responsiveness to God's grace. She had a rare faith that saw beyond circumstances, a faith that worked by love and grasped the promises of God as though they were a doorknob that need only be turned to open the treasure house of His freely offered gifts.

Elijah arrived in this widow's town on the very day she had been reduced to her last food supplies. Following this final meal that she would make for herself and her son, she expected the slow, gnawing process of starvation to claim their lives. What more severe test could she be given than that of sacrificing her last meager rations to this alien migrant?

Because she honored the God of Israel and believed His word, she did as Elijah requested. What a blessing she would have missed had she let cold human reason or self-interest overrule her faith in the Lord! Did Elijah ask this humble widow to feed him first because he regarded his needs as more important than her own? No. He already had ample evidence of God's ability to provide for *his* needs. How could he forget the ravens? Elijah came not as a freeloader but as an undetected benefactor, making his request at God's direction (see 1 Kings 17:9, 10).

Elijah's ministry to the Sidonian widow gives us valuable insight into his balanced nature. Not obsessed with the rigorous demands of his mission, Elijah had a very personal and tenderhearted care for people. How different this is from self-appointed prophets, who hold themselves above everyone else. Their mission is sublime! The world owes them homage, support, and unquestioning deference! Such egocentricity bears no resemblance to the spirit of God's true prophets, all of whom have had a servant-spirit that was attentive to the needs of others. Elijah was no exception. His request that the widow make him a loaf first was not selfishly motivated. It was a divinely appointed test to see whether she would trust God enough to give *Him* first place. Her compliance, and God's special blessing on her as a reward for her faithfulness, should indelibly remind us that when we seek first the kingdom of God and His righteousness, He will grant us everything we need, according to His riches in glory (Matt. 6:33; Phil. 4:19).

In our spiritual experience we all frequently face analogous tests. Take tithing and Sabbath observance, for example. Satan strives to make these two faith-commitments seem impossible or severely impracticable. *What, give God ten percent of my income as tithe and then an offering above that, when I can't even afford to pay all my bills now? Impossible, unreasonable, absurd!* And yet how many who keep this covenant with God have found Him to be true to His promise to open up the windows of heaven and pour out a blessing, so large that we haven't room to contain it in our own lives (see Prov. 3:9, 10; Mal. 3:10-12). Thus we are stimulated and inspired by His blessing, both material and spiritual, to share the overflow with others.

*What, keep the Sabbath and lose my job or forfeit my promotion? Never! God knows my position, I simply can't obey without suffering earthly loss and ridicule from my friends and family. Surely He wouldn't want me to make such an unreasonable sacrifice over something so minor as the Sabbath?* Multitudes wrongly reason thus, to their profound loss. They fear to be partners with God because they don't seriously believe that His covenant-calling is real.

Yet millions of Sabbath-keeping Christians worldwide have discovered that God is able to honor those who honor Him and cause them to ride upon the high places of the earth, through the indescribably rich blessings of His fellowship with them on the Sabbath (see Isa. 58:13, 14). Whatever they may lose temporally is more than compensated for spiritually. Nor does God allow all Sabbath keepers, even prior to earth's final test, to suffer financial loss for their faith and obedience.[2] Many prosper more as Sabbath keepers than in former days when they neglected God's holy day. But whatever the effect on our material circumstances, the true motive for Sabbath keeping is love for our Creator who, because He made and sustains us, has rightful primacy in our lives.

Those who, as a fixed principle, obey God will find that in times of extraordinary trial and need, "the barrel of meal shall not waste, neither shall the cruse of oil fail, until the day the Lord sendeth rain upon the earth" (1 Kings 17:14, KJV). As God proved true to His promise on behalf of the widow of Zarephath, so He will now to all whose love for Him leads to unquestioning obedience in all circumstances. How overjoyed this woman must have been by God's goodness and mercy in answer to her simple faith! Yet every day she had to rely on God and renew her trust in Him for daily provision. Her barrel was never miraculously filled to the top, nor did her cruet run over; both vessels always contained just enough for each day's sustenance. This taught her the lesson of daily dependence and trust.

But a still greater test lay before this widow. Her son fell sick and died, leaving her alone in the world. In this tragedy she did what many people do in similar circumstances: She blamed God. She did this indirectly by attributing her misfortune to Elijah's presence as a guest in her home. But Elijah did not take offense. He empathized with her in her grief, and God answered his earnest plea on the widow's behalf by restoring her son to life. *Elijah* did not resurrect the boy, only Jesus, who has the keys to the grave and death could do that. He is the Resurrection and the Life. But by faith, Elijah had a strong connection with the Lifegiver, and so his petition was answered.

In this we see convincing evidence that Elijah was not a man who reveled in desolation and doom. He valued the preciousness of human life and welcomed the opportunity to be a channel of blessing to someone. His words and works were as a balm of Gilead to the afflicted widow. What a clear lesson that leaves for all who would be reformers today. God never assigns His followers a work of mere moralizing, unconnected with positive action. Real reformers are animated with a spirit of service that delights in performing acts of mercy, not to obtain fame but to be a blessing to others. They watch for opportunities to enrich and ennoble the lives of all who will accept their service. "This is pure and undefiled religion in the sight of our God and Father, to visit orphans and widows in their distress, and to keep oneself unstained by the world" (James 1:27, NASB).

Those who have a great burden to denounce wrong wherever they see it, especially in the church, but have little inclination to help the suffering and needy, are on a self-appointed mission that wins no endorsement from heaven.[3] They are not ambassadors for Christ but ambushers for the accuser the brethren. Let us determine not to get caught up in such a dreary role but, like the apostle Paul, learn how to labor unselfishly that we may present every man perfect in Christ, not because we have badgered anyone into righteousness—an impossibility—but have worked and prayed in the spirit of the Redeemer to make Him savingly known. Stern, officious men never win anyone to Christ, but the quiet touch of grace has brought more people to salvation than anyone can estimate this side of paradise.[4]

Those who serve in the spirit of their Master do not trumpet their deeds, but all heaven rejoices and sings over their work and blesses it as abundantly as it blessed the widow's faith and Elijah's prayers. God's prophets are comparatively few, but those who receive "a prophet in the name of a prophet [i.e., in the name of the true God for whom the prophet speaks] shall receive a prophet's reward" (Matt. 10:41).

After Elijah's almost halcyon interlude in heathendom, it was time to return to Israel. But a foreboding question looms over the hills and valleys south of Sidon—would Israel be ready to receive its prophet?

*Questions for Discussion and Reflection*

1. Why did Jesus refer to the widow of Zarephath (Sarepta)? What lesson was He trying to teach by her example? Why did His

own townspeople who heard Him then take offense? Luke 4:25, 26. See the whole story in Luke 4:14-30.

2. What does Elijah's presence among the Baal-worshiping people of Sidon say about God's attitude toward the heathen world? How do you think Elijah's sojourn among them affected their lives?

3. How do you suppose Elijah's experience with the widow of Zarephath affected his own spiritual experience and his feelings toward Gentiles?

4. Have you ever been in a position where it seemed that by placing God's requirements ahead of your own immediate needs, you would suffer great loss or difficulty? What did you do, and what was the outcome? What lesson(s) did you learn from this experience?

---

1. *Prophets and Kings*, 129.

2. According to prophecy, someday all Sabbath keepers will be brought to a test similar to that of the Sidonian widow. Obedience to God will bring them face to face with absolute deprivation of all earthly goods and the peril of death. See Rev. 13:11-18; cf. Rev. 12:17; Ezek. 20:12, 20. But God promises to vindicate His people who face this excruciating test with loyalty to Him. See Daniel 7 and 12.

3. "We are threads in the great web of humanity, and, as such, related with each other. Our life leaves upon the minds of others impressions which will be transferred even into eternity. Angels take note of our works, of our words, of the spirit which actuates us. Those who desire to reform others must begin the reformation in their own hearts, and show that they have acquired kindliness and humility of heart in the school of Christ. Those who have charge of others must learn first to master themselves, to refrain from blunt expressions and exaggerated censure." (*The Upward Look*, 59).

4. See *Testimonies for the Church*, 5:349, 350; *The Upward Look*, 120.

# CHAPTER
# 5

# Elijah Summons Ahab

During his three-and-a-half-year sojourn in voluntary exile, first by the brook Cherith and later in Sidon, Elijah waited patiently on the Lord. But this was by no means an idle or fruitless season for the prophet. He continued praying fervently that Israel, through their humbling punishment by drought, would repent. God was withholding the rain, parching the earth, until the people were prepared to recognize that they had chosen to live in a moral desert, destitute of the Spirit, when they could have been drinking spiritually of the water of life and had the joy of being channels of that living water to the world (see Ezek. 47:1-12; John 7:35-37; Heb. 13:8). Selfishness and sensuality had cut off this bountiful supply and spiritually turned their nation into a Sahara.

Now the time had come for God to reveal Himself once more to His people and offer them strong incentive to give up their idols in exchange for the joys of true salvation. But this change would not be easy, because those who sin in direct violation of God's revealed light do not readily turn from spiritual darkness. They barricade themselves in the false security of their illusions. Truth is frightening to the slaves of falsehood, especially when falsehood has achieved the status of established religious belief and custom, as Baal worship had done in Israel.

That's why forceful measures were needed to liberate the nation. And God had found a man who was willing to be His agent of change. Elijah. His very name, meaning, *My God Is Jah*, declares his mission. Jah (Yahweh), because He is the sole Creator, should be everybody's God, and certainly He should be the God of all who profess to know, worship, and serve Him.

But how were God's wandering, rebellious people to be brought back to worshiping Him in spirit and in truth? What more practical and convincing way than to test the claims of Baal against those of the Creator? If Baal was in charge of the elements, let him prove it by sending rain in all its desperately needed abundance. But if Baal were powerless to do this, would the true God deign to send this undeserved blessing to restore people to a knowledge of His truth and love? Assuredly, He would. His promise was, "When I shut up heaven and there is no rain, . . . if My people who are called by My name will humble themselves, and pray and seek My face, and turn from their wicked ways, then I will hear from heaven, and will forgive their sin and heal their land" (2 Chron. 7:14).

And so, "after many days," the word of the Lord came to Elijah, "Go, show thyself unto Ahab; and I will send rain upon the earth." Without hesitation, or fear of personal risk, Elijah "went to show himself to Ahab" (1Kings 18:1-3, KJV). On his way southward to Samaria, Elijah met up with Obadiah, Ahab's God-fearing servant, who was roaming the countryside in search of water, while the king, on the same quest, went in another direction.

Although steward to Ahab, Obadiah's paramount loyalty was to God. He "had taken one hundred prophets and hidden them, fifty to a cave, and had fed them with bread and water" (1 Kings 18:4). How easy it would be to cynically observe that Obadiah had no business working for so corrupt a king, in a court that was blatantly apostate. But that's only an opinion. Obadiah, at the risk of his life, was serving God and upholding His cause amid desperately bad conditions. Israel would have been far worse off if Obadiah had abandoned the court. We should avoid forming hasty judgments about the occupations others pursue and recognize that God has His Obadiahs today in government service and other secular positions. They are there to preserve and promote His cause.

Astonished to see Elijah, Obadiah quickly dismounted his horse and falling prostrate on the ground, asked, " 'Is that you, my lord Elijah?'

"And he answered him, 'It is I. Go, tell your master, 'Elijah is here' " (1 Kings 18:7, 8).

But this charge frightened Obadiah. He feared that before he could lead the king to Elijah, the prophet would disappear, and Ahab in his petulance would then turn upon Obadiah and kill him. But Elijah assured him that he would present himself to the king that day. So Obadiah found Ahab and brought him to the prophet.

Ahab wanted to kill Elijah on the spot, but fear restrained him. After all, might not God protect his prophet and punish the king the way He did Jeroboam by causing his arm to wither when he stretched it out against one of God's prophets? Fearful and angry, Ahab approached the prophet, and flung out the words, "Is that you, O troubler of Israel?" (v. 17). But Elijah was not the cause of Israel's trouble. He hurled the imputation back on the king, who was the real source of the trouble. Prophets who declare God's judgment are not to blame, but the transgressors who provoke His judgment.

At the end of time God's people who faithfully declare His final warning to the world will foolishly be held accountable for the calamities they warned against under divine authority. It's an age-old sin to punish the messenger for bringing unwelcome words of warning or judgment, when the proper response would be to heed the message and repent.

> Those who refuse to receive reproof and to be corrected will manifest enmity, malice, and hatred against the instrument that God has used. They will leave no means untried to cast stigma upon the one who bore to them the message. They will feel as did Ahab toward Elijah, that God's servant is the one who is the hindrance, the curse.[1]

This is as true today as it was in Elijah's time. Many, even in the Christian church, feel that reproof or censure of any kind is cruelly judgmental. They have little use for Paul's exhortation to Timothy,

"Preach the word! Be ready in season and out of season. Convince, rebuke, exhort with all longsuffering and teaching" (2 Tim. 4:2). Why this modern-day resistance to plain speaking from the Word of God? "For the time will come when they will not endure sound doctrine, but according to their own desires, because they have itching ears, they will heap up for themselves teachers; and they will turn their ears away from the truth, and be turned aside to fables" (vss. 3, 4). This will lead many to deny the signs of the times and pin their hopes on fanciful dreams that quiet the conscience and blind the heart to the issues of God's judgment upon a wicked world.

Jesus foretold that calamities in nature and society would multiply shortly before His return. These calamities follow humanity's widespread disobedience to God's law, and Satan's consequent freedom to harass and plague earth's populace (see Isa. 24:4-6; Zech. 7:8-12). "And then the great deceiver will persuade men that those who serve God are causing these evils. The class that have provoked the displeasure of Heaven will charge all their troubles against those whose obedience to God's commandments is a perpetual reproof to transgressors."[2] In a later chapter we will examine in detail the implications of this malign movement against God's faithful witnesses.

Elijah got directly to the source of the problem. Israel was in trouble not because of Elijah's prophecy but because of their sins as a nation. "The curse never comes without a reason" (Prov. 26:2, free translation). So Elijah answered Ahab, "I have not troubled Israel, but you and your father's house have, in that you have forsaken the commandments of the Lord, and you have followed the Baals. Now therefore, send and gather all Israel to me on Mount Carmel, the four hundred and fifty prophets of Baal, and the four hundred prophets of Asherah, who eat at Jezebel's table" (1 Kings 18:18, 19).

Elijah spoke for God, and King Ahab, as though he were the subject and Elijah the monarch, hastened to obey the order. Elijah's faithfulness in bearing so strong a testimony showed rare courage. Holding the honor of God supreme, he did not evade telling the truth or stoop to flatter the king.

Today there is need of the voice of stern rebuke; for grievous sins have separated the people from God. . . . The smooth sermons so often preached make no lasting impression; the trumpet does not give a certain sound. Men are not cut to the heart by the plain, sharp truths of God's word.

There are many professed Christians who, if they should express their real feelings, would say, What need is there of speaking so plainly? They might as well ask, Why need John the Baptist have said to the Pharisees, 'O generation of vipers, who hath warned you to flee from the wrath to come?' Luke 3:7. Why need he have provoked the anger of Herodias by telling Herod that it was unlawful for him to live with his brother's wife? The forerunner of Christ lost his life by his plain speaking. Why could he not have moved along without incurring the displeasure of those who were living in sin?

So men who should be standing as faithful guardians of God's law have argued, till policy has taken the place of faithfulness, and sin is allowed to go unreproved. When will the voice of faithful rebuke be heard once more in the church?[3]

This is a probing question, and, as a minister of the gospel, it makes me think whether I have the integrity and the courage—and most of all the love for Christ and for people—to bear a faithful testimony, even at the cost of losing favor among some of those whom I am appointed to shepherd. All counsel should be given in kindness and love, but it should not evade stating necessary truths that are hard for our fallen natures to bear.

As pastors it is our responsibility to hold the honor of God and the salvation of souls uppermost. May God make us who are in ministry faithful and keep us from cowardice and self-interest in serving Him, and especially from giving smooth, soothing words when we should be warning souls who are in spiritual danger. It is sometimes hard to carry out this responsibility, because people can be easily offended, especially in this age of hypersensitive egos and feel-good theology that downplays obedience to God's law while invoking His love as an excuse for sin (see Matt. 24:10; 2 Tim. 4:1-5).

Would that every minister might realize the sacredness of his office and the holiness of his work, and show the courage that Elijah showed! As divinely appointed messengers, ministers are in a position of awful responsibility. They are to "reprove, rebuke, exhort with all long-suffering." 2 Timothy 4:2. In Christ's stead they are to labor as verified stewards of the mysteries of heaven, encouraging the obedient and warning the disobedient. With them worldly policy is to have no weight. Never are they to swerve from the path in which Jesus has bidden them walk. They are to go forward in faith, remembering that they are surrounded by a cloud of witnesses. They are not to speak their own words, but words which One greater than the potentates of earth has bidden them speak. Their message is to be, 'Thus saith the Lord.' God calls for men like Elijah, Nathan, and John the Baptist—men who will bear His message with faithfulness, regardless of the consequences; men who will speak the truth bravely, though it call for the sacrifice of all they have.

God cannot use men who, in time of peril, when the strength, courage, and influence of all are needed, are afraid to take a firm stand for the right. He calls for men who will do faithful battle against wrong, warring against principalities and powers, against the rulers of the darkness of this world, against spiritual wickedness in high places. It is to such as these that He will speak the words: "Well done, good and faithful servant; . . . enter thou into the joy of thy Lord." Matthew 25:23.[4]

This passage should make us all consider: Do I want a minister who will faithfully speak truth that brings conviction to me when I need to change my ways and come up to higher ground? And if I reject such a ministry, how will that affect my salvation?

*Questions for Discussion and Reflection*

1. Why do those who reject light from heaven end up in greater

darkness than those who have not had the light? John 3:19-21; 12:35-41; Acts 28:23-28; cf. Isa. 30:8-15.

2. Obadiah was a faithful servant of God. How can this fact be reconciled with his also being the chief minister of Ahab, a wicked, apostate king? Ps. 75:6, 7; Dan. 2:21, 47; 1 Cor. 9:19-23.3. How is it possible to bear a straight testimony for the Lord without being offensive or seemingly self-righteous? How is God's cause affected if His servants are too cowardly or cautious to plainly speak His word?

4. How do you relate to reproof from God's Word? Consider Prov. 1:23; 6:23; 10:17; 13:18; 15:5, 10, 31, 32; 17:10; 29:1.

---

1. *Review and Herald*, 8 January 1884.

2. *The Great Controversy*, 590.

3. *Prophets and Kings*, 140, 141.

4. Ibid, 142.

# CHAPTER

# 6

# Elijah on Carmel

**G**od had long been preparing Israel for this day. It was a day of reckoning, of confrontation, to sweep away falsehood and folly and to restore the truth in all its original power and beauty.

Standing before Ahab, Elijah gave the word of command, " 'Send and gather all Israel to me on Mount Carmel, the four hundred and fifty prophets of Baal, and the four hundred prophets of Asherah, who eat at Jezebel's table' " (1 Kings 18:18, 19). Elijah spoke for God, and Ahab unresistingly obeyed. The sweeping summons flew quickly through his realm, stirring up anxious forebodings among the people. All Israel knew that its national religious life had grown corrupt, deviating from the purity of God's laws and holy way of worship; yet they had permitted this decline without protest. Thus the people assembled as to a vast arraignment to hear the sentence of God. They must also have sensed that something momentous would occur to change the present order of religious life, which had proven an absolute failure.

Mount Carmel overlooked a wide expanse of country; its heights were visible from many parts of Israel. This mountain was a center of Baal worship, a stronghold of defiance toward God, and negation of true worship.[1] How fitting that the confrontation should be here!

As the prophets of Baal climbed the heights of Carmel the question that bothered them most was, "Why weren't the gods of Baal able to prove Elijah a false prophet?" After all, it hadn't rained in Israel for three years, an unprecedented drought for that region. Moreover, everyone knew that the rain had been withheld according to Elijah's word. Now, what could the "gods" of Baal do, and what would Elijah's God do? It was precisely to settle this question that Elijah had called for this vast convocation of Israel and her pagan religious leaders.

With all the pomp and splendor their quaking hearts could muster, Jezebel's prophets and priests gathered in company with the king and his entourage. Elijah stood alone against this imposing assemblage, having no desire to appear as though he was on the popular side. Without visible allies, Elijah nevertheless stood in the majority with God and all the hosts of heaven. This knowledge braced him for his task.

Often during this prolonged drought the pagan clergy had met on Mount Carmel to practice their wild tarantellas and incantations, summoning Baal to send rain. But "are there any among the idols of the nations that can cause rain?" (Jer. 14:22). At least some of these religious leaders must have recognized the fraudulence of their claims, but their positions were materially profitable, and the people were easily deceived. To have their powers put to the ultimate test was the last thing these cult leaders wanted, yet, because of Elijah, they could not evade this dreaded confrontation.

Without fear or shame Elijah stands before the people. He knows his mission—to bring the people back to the Lord and abolish Baal worship in Israel. This called for an informed choice on their part and moral courage that wouldn't stagger in the face of demonic seduction and the natural bent of the human heart toward fanciful religion that pampers carnality. True religion is not only doctrinally sound, it also restores its participants to the image of God. It transforms character and purifies from sin. It reinstates people to the full dignity of membership in the family of God. This is what God wanted for His people. This is why He commissioned Elijah to carry out so bold and blazing a charge.

Elijah's face reflects the authority of his commission. "The awful solemnity in the looks of the prophet gives him the appearance of one standing in the presence of the Lord God of Israel. The condition of Israel in their apostasy demands a firm demeanor, stern speech, and commanding authority. God prepares the message to fit the time and occasion."[2] In suspense the people await his words. Surveying the vast assembly, Elijah asks in trumpetlike tones, "How long will you falter between two opinions? If the Lord is God, follow Him; but if Baal, follow him" (1Kings 18:21).

Elijah's probing call reveals that Israel was in a state of confused ambivalence. Teetering between two ways, they had not wholly cast off the religion of their fathers. They simply wished to have an updated version of it, an "improved" species of Yahweh worship hybridized with contemporary values and tastes. But they were operating under the influence of the age-old lie that truth is enhanced by departure from God's plain instructions.

It remains eternally true that light cannot commune with darkness and righteousness can have no fellowship with unrighteousness, nor Christ with Belial (see 2 Cor. 6:14, 15). God's true worship was designed to elevate and ennoble humanity, to set people free from the corrupting influences of superstition, sensuality, and priestcraft and to reveal the work of faith by the liberating power of the Cross. It was heaven's work then, as it is now, to direct people to the Lamb of God who takes away the sin of the world.

Elijah's question cut the people to their hearts. So long had they been paralyzed by the effects of apostasy and accustomed to rejecting divine counsel and conviction that it was hard for them to break loose from the chains of spiritual slavery. Too stultified and numb to take a stand, they stood mute before Elijah.

What astonishing deception and fearful blindness had, like a dark cloud, covered Israel! This blindness and apostasy had not closed about them suddenly; it had come upon them gradually as they had not heeded the word of reproof and warning which the Lord had sent to them because of their pride and their sins. And now, in this fearful crisis, in the presence of the idolatrous priests and the apostate king, they remained neutral. If God abhors one sin above another, of which His people are guilty, it is doing nothing in case of an emergency. Indifference and neutrality in a religious crisis is regarded of God as a grievous crime and equal to the very worst type of hostility against God. [3]

Does this statement seem too strong? What if Peter and John had not said to the enemies of the gospel, who tried to stop their preaching, "Whether it is right in the sight of God to listen to you more than to God, you judge. For we cannot but speak the thing which we have seen and heard" (Acts 4:19, 20)? Had they cooperated with the Pharisees' unrighteous demand, the gospel would have suffered a severe setback from the outset, because enfeebling terror would have gripped the church.

What if Patrick Henry had not valiantly declared, "Give me liberty, or give me death"? What if the signers of the Declaration of Independence had feared to show their colors and sign the fateful document? Wouldn't the cause of American Independence have faltered, perhaps even failed?

What if on December 1, 1955, Rosa Parks had moved to the back of the bus in Montgomery, Alabama, in deference to the driver's bigoted demand? And if the black citizens of Montgomery had chosen to remain neutral, would the civil-rights movement have marched forth so nobly or found a better rallying point for the pursuit of justice and eradication of Jim Crow laws?[4]

What if the Romanians of Timisoara had not bravely stood up to the brutal regime of the dictator Ceaucescu, thus sparking national resistance; would their nation have been liberated to hear the gospel and enjoy its present freedom?

Lack of moral courage and prolonged neutrality in Europe made it possible for the psychopath Hitler to control Germany for nearly fifteen years and almost destroy civilization in the process. Neutrality has made it possible for many evils to flourish in our world and for many blessings to be trampled underfoot without a murmur of protest. Neutrality does not clothe the naked, feed the starving, free the oppressed, or heal the wounds of strife. Neutrality in the face of duty to God is bland betrayal and passive treason. Scripture declares, "You have given a banner to those who fear You, that it may be *displayed* because of the truth" (Ps. 60:4). Truth deserves to be upheld with boldness and good cheer, especially in those times and places where it is least honored (see Ps. 119:126-128).

All who stand for the right, to honor God, can declare in the spirit of David, "The Lord is my light and my salvation; whom shall I fear? The Lord is the strength of my life; of whom shall I be afraid? . . . Though an army should encamp against me, my heart shall not fear" (Ps. 27:1, 3).

In solitary grandeur Elijah stands before all, the fearful, the defiant, the skeptical, the dismayed. He proposes a simple test, so reasonable and decisive that none can question or evade it. "Elijah said to the people, 'I alone am left a prophet of the Lord; but Baal's prophets are four hundred and fifty men. Therefore let them give us two bulls; and let them choose one bull for themselves, cut it in pieces, and lay it on the wood, but put no fire under it; and I will prepare the other bull, and lay it on the wood, but put no fire under it. Then you call on the name of your gods, and I will call on the name of the Lord; and the God who answers by fire, He is God.' So all the people answered and said, 'It is well spoken.' Now Elijah said to the prophets of Baal, 'Choose one bull for yourselves and prepare it first, for you are many; and call on the name of your god, but put no fire under it' " (1 Kings 18:22-25).

How could the priests do anything but accept the conditions? Elijah has offered them every advantage to vindicate themselves and their god. Wearing a mask of confidence, they proceed with the plan, while quaking inside. They slaughter their bull, place him on their altar, and then begin their weird incantations and wailing chants to invoke Baal's power. No fire comes down to consume the sacrifice. No celestial voice is heard, no supernatural sights appear. Enraged and desperate, they intensify their efforts.

In the midst of their frantic gyrations and raucous yelping, Elijah's voice rings out in undisguised mockery, "Cry aloud, for he is a god; either he is meditating, or he is busy, or he is on a journey, or perhaps he is sleeping and must be awakened" (vs. 27).[5] So the priests throw themselves into calling on Baal with heightened frenzy. Whirling about their altar like dervishes, they bellow, shout, and shriek themselves hoarse. Cavorting and leaping, they gash themselves with knives, as if to make a sacrifice of themselves, thus illustrating the extremes to which the carnal heart is willing to go in attempting to "gain" divine favor while avoiding God's authority and grace.

We would like to think of this kind of foolishness as belonging exclusively to the realm of paganism. But a species of false Christianity stalks about closely resembling Baal-worship in spirit, if not in outward appearance.

> Whenever professed Christians are constantly flaunting their leaves of profession before the eyes of others, there is no real fruit to the glory of God. Their religious life and experience seem satisfactory to themselves. They have exaggerated emotions, effusive expressions of fervor, and highest exaltations. Their religion consists largely in feeling and excitement. There is very little in their souls that corresponds to their profession of faith. Self is their ideal of perfection. They value more the outward impression they make on others than the inner life which is hidden with Christ in God.[6]

From early morning until the time of the evening sacrifice the votaries of Baal keep up their frenetic spectacle. "How gladly would Satan, who fell like lightning from heaven, come to help those whom he has deceived, whose minds he has controlled, and who are fully devoted to his service; but Jehovah has set Satan's bounds. He has restrained his power, and all his devices cannot convey one spark to Baal's altars."[7] How desperately the cavorting priests would have liked to use a trick to start a fire on their altar, to make it appear as though Baal had answered their invocations. But Elijah and the people had them under close scrutiny, making such a deception impossible. Finally the priests of Baal fling themselves on the ground, voiceless, gasping, spent, and bleeding.

"Then Elijah said to all the people, 'Come near to me.' So all the people came near to him. And he repaired the altar of the Lord that was broken down. And Elijah took twelve stones, according to the number of the tribes of the sons of Jacob, to whom the word of the Lord had come, saying, 'Israel shall be your name.' Then with the stones he built an altar in the name of the Lord; and he made a trench around the altar large enough to hold about two seahs [15 liters] of seed. And he put the wood in order, cut the bull in pieces, and laid it on the wood, and said, 'Fill four water pots with water, and pour it on the burnt sacrifice and on the wood.' Then he said, 'Do it a second time,' and they did it a second time; and he said, 'Do it a third time,' and they did it a third time. So the water ran all around the altar; and he also filled the trench with water. And it came to pass, at the time of the offering of the evening sacrifice, that Elijah the prophet came near and said, 'Lord God of Abraham, Isaac, and Israel, let it be known this day that You are God in Israel, and that I am Your servant, and that I have done all these things at Your word. Hear me, O Lord, hear me, that this people may know that You are the Lord God, and that you have turned their hearts back to you again.'

"Then the fire of the Lord fell and consumed the burnt sacrifice, and the wood and the stones and the dust, and it licked up the water that was in the trench. Now when all the people saw it, they fell on their faces: and the people said, 'The Lord, He is God! The Lord, He is God!' " (1 Kings 18:30-39).

This narrative is simple, unadorned, but supercharged with meaning. For in many ways it represents the apex of Elijah's message and mission, displayed between two eternally conflicting systems of worship, Satan's versus the Lord's. Epitomizing the controversy between Christ and Satan, this confrontation on Carmel pungently testifies that truth eventually triumphs over error, and righteousness over evil. It is a historic metaphor for all reforms, especially those carried out under forbidding conditions in which evil predominates.

From Elijah's work on Carmel we learn:
- There is a day of ultimate reckoning (1 Kings 18:17-19). God does not allow sin to go forever unchallenged and unchecked.
- We need to choose resolutely whom we will serve and not vacillate (1 Kings 18:21). God has given us the power of choice; it is ours to use (Deut. 30:19, 20).

44

- He will fully support us in making the right choice no matter how great the obstacles and the opposition (2 Tim. 4:16-18; Rev. 15:2-4).
- It is our privilege and duty to stand courageously for the truth (1 Kings 18:21-24).
- God's law is sacred, inviolable (1 Kings 18:18; cf. Ps. 119:126-128, 142, 151).
- The utter vanity of the world's approach to spiritual revival (1 Kings 18:25-29).
- True revival is free from extravagance, folly, and noisy show (1 Kings 18:30).
- True reformers have a ministry of reconciliation, not to the *status quo*, but to God and His will  (1 Kings 18:30).
- True revival resorts to no gimmicks, no humanly devised methods for success; it is carried out in the name of the Lord and in a manner that befits the dignity of His name and word (1 Kings 18:31-35).
- True revival is steeped in prayer; it is neither frivolous nor legalistic but is well-defined in its aim: the honor of God and the salvation of souls (1 Kings 18:37; cf. Ps. 85:6-13).
- True revival is crowned with the fiery baptism of the Holy Spirit that exalts Christ and His righteousness, illuminating the power of His sacrifice (1 Kings 18:38; cf. Matt. 3:11; Acts 2:3).
- True revival brings people back to God, it does not merely generate excitement without sober decisions in compliance with the will of God (1 Kings 18:39).
- True revival purges idolatry and worldliness from the church (1 Kings 18:40).

Think of this confrontation on Carmel in the light of Malachi's prophecy, "Behold I will send you Elijah the prophet before the coming of the great and dreadful day of the Lord. And he will turn the hearts of the fathers of the children and the hearts of the children to their fathers . . ." (Mal. 4:5, 6). This speaks of a future work, which parallels that of Elijah. In what way did the first, literal Elijah turn the hearts of God's people in such a positive direction? Consider Elijah's prayer: "Lord God of Abraham, Isaac, and Israel, let it be known this day that you are God in Israel. . . . Hear me, O Lord, hear me, that this people may know that You are the Lord God, and that You have turned *their heart* back to You again" (1 Kings 18:37, 38, emphasis added).

Elijah was not a stony moralist seeking to reinstate an *outward show* of godliness in Israel. He sincerely longed for the reconversion of his people. He realized that heart religion was the only kind possessing value. Moreover, he saw that *God* must reclaim the heart and that human persuasion alone was not an adequate source of revival and reformation. Elijah also sought to bring the people back to an appreciation of the Atonement. All that he did on Carmel centered on the substitutionary sacrifice that prefigured Calvary. That's why he repaired the ancient Israelite altar and specified the consuming of the true sacrifice by miraculous fire as a conclusive demonstration that Yahweh is superior to all pagan gods.

No wonder that eight centuries later Elijah was chosen along with Moses to join Christ on the Mount of Transfiguration and speak with Him concerning His decease that He should accomplish at Jerusalem! Elijah was a man to whom the Messiah's redeeming sacrifice was a subject of central interest even during his earthly life. This enlightened awareness gave substance, grace, and authority to his mission.

Consider also how nobly Elijah's deportment and reverent prayer contrasted with the bizarre gesticulations and shrieks of Baal's representatives. God's definitive answer in consuming the sacrifice with the stones of the altar and all the water that drenched the site brought the people to recognition and repentance. By failing to acknowledge the power of God even after this striking demonstration, the prophets and priests of Baal showed themselves ripe for destruction. They were dealt with according to the theocratic rules that God had established for His chosen people (see Deut. 18:10, 11, 20).

We live in an age in which Baal worship of a more sophisticated but no less immoral character flourishes, and therefore Elijah's example of courage and fidelity resounds with significance for us today. We are to stand for God and His truth, not with harsh militancy but with fixed loyalty and unflinching courage. Like Elijah we are to pray that God will turn the hearts of the rebellious and the deceived back to

Himself and will reveal Himself in power and grace to those who walk in darkness.

One day a worldly businessman was traveling on a train in Philadelphia. A boy boarded the train and started reading a religious paper. Thinking to have a little fun at the boy's expense, the man jovially asked, "Do you go to church, little fellow?" "I sure do," he replied, scrutinizing the man's derisive expression. "Tell me, sonny, where God is, and I'll give you an apple." The boy looked sharply at the man and shot back, "Mister, I'll give you a whole barrel of apples if you'll tell me where God is not." In that instant he showed the dash and decisiveness of Elijah in standing upright for the Lord. Let no one ever shame or mock you out of your faith. God honors those who revere Him and makes their mountain to stand strong, as they firmly stand for His truth, while fully trusting in His grace.[8]

As we shall see in the next chapter, Elijah and God had a further work to do on Carmel before the day ended.

*Questions for Discussion and Reflection*

1. Why did Elijah order the people and the leaders of Baal worship to gather on Mount Carmel? Was it to punish Israel or to liberate them from the degrading effects of Baal worship?

2. What evidence do you find in 1 Kings 18 that Elijah stood for the commandments of God and the faith of Jesus? How does Elijah's stand correlate with the position and beliefs of God's last day witnesses? See Rev. 14:12.

3. When Elijah challenged the Israelites to choose between serving Baal and the Lord, why did they say nothing? Think of at least three reasons. If you had been there, what would you have said? Why?

4. If Elijah had not been so convincing a representative of true spirituality, how would his challenge to Baal worship have turned out on Mount Carmel? How important is it that you be converted to Christ

47

and His gospel before you can lead others to a saving connection with God?

---

1. *Prophets and Kings*, 144. Carmel means "garden" or "orchard," which indicates its exceptional fruitfulness and beauty during the growing season (see Isa. 35:2; Song of Solomon 7:5). Elijah's choice of this mountain ridge related to its being a stronghold of Baal worship. Carmel's outdoor altars and groves were devoted to idolatrous worship, which had displaced the worship of God, as signified by the ruined altar of Yahweh, which Elijah repaired (1 Kings 18:30).

2. *Testimonies for the Church*, 3:279.

3. Ibid., 281.

4. The Montgomery bus boycott of 1956, a movement of peaceful protest, constitutes one of the towering episodes in the history of civil rights.

5. It would be inappropriate to criticize Elijah for mocking the priests as they performed their ludicrous antics with such desperate seriousness. He was acting in his office as the Lord's prophet and doubtless was prompted to expose the absurdity of their worship. But we are not to take our cue from this in speaking derisively of those who teach or receive error. Christ is our perfect example, and He was never sarcastic or satirical in his dealings with anyone.

"Be sure that you do not make the word of the Lord offensive. We long to see reforms, and because we do not see that which we desire, an evil spirit is too often allowed to cast drops of gall into our cup, and thus others are embittered. By our ill-advised words their spirit is chafed, and they are stirred to rebellion.

"Every sermon you preach, every article you write, may be all true; but one drop of gall in it will be poison to the hearer or the reader. Because of that drop of poison, one will discard all your good and acceptable words. Another will feed on the poison; for he loves such harsh words; he follows your example, and talks just as you talk. Thus the evil is multiplied.

"Those who present the eternal principles of truth need the holy oil emptied from the two olive branches into the heart. This will flow forth in words that will reform, but not exasperate. The truth is to be spoken in love. Then the Lord Jesus by His Spirit will supply the force and the power. That is His work" (*Testimonies for the Church*, 6:122, 123).

Perhaps Elijah's mockery, so uncharacteristic of the prophets, is a foretype of the Lord's declaration found in Psalm 2:1-4; cf. Psalm 37:10-17.

6. *That I May Know Him*, 133.

7. *Testimonies for the Church*, 3:282, 283. God did not permit Satan to ignite the sacrifice to Baal on Carmel, but in these last days God's people will have to face a closer test than did the ancient Israelites. For Satan will be permitted to generate what appears to be heavenly fire, sent in support of demonic miracles and the mark of the beast (Rev. 13:11-15; cf. Matt. 24:24). God's people will find their strength not

in countermiracles but in the sealing power of full adherence to His covenant.

8. Ps. 30:7; Rom. 5:1, 2; 1 Cor. 15:1, 2; Eph. 6:10-13. When Jesus invites His victorious people into His Kingdom, He shall say, "You have washed your robes in My blood, stood stiffly for My truth, enter in" *(Early Writings*, 17).

# CHAPTER

# 7

# And Then Came the Rain

**N**ow that the spell of Baal worship had been broken from the people's hearts and a work of reformation had begun, it was time for the Lord to send rain to the parched and weary land. Under Elijah's bold leadership, the people had at least begun to meet God's conditions (see Leviticus 26:3-5; Deuteronomy 11:13-16; 2 Chronicles 7:13-15). But the rain was not theirs automatically by right. As with all the bounties of life, God's promise of rain was a gift, not a debt. But *we* are indebted to *Him* for His gifts. We have no blessing that we have not received and for which we do not owe God thanks and allegiance. Elijah knew this and turned again to God for His intervention in this matter.

He was not only a man of decisive action but also of prevailing prayer. "The natural cooperates with the supernatural. It is a part of God's plan to grant us, in answer to the prayer of faith, that which He would not bestow did we not thus ask."[1] Consider this statement in the light of James's admonition, "Ye have not, because ye ask not;" and Jesus' assurance, "If you then being evil, know how to give good gifts to your children, how much more shall your Father which is in heaven give good things to them that ask him?" (James 4:2; Matt. 7:11, KJV).

No hindrance stood in the way of Elijah's faith. He was acting in

God's strength and saw clearly the next step in His plan—the rain was to fall, not a light sprinkling but a rich abundance of rain. So while the evening sky was yet cloudless and the sun arced westward, Elijah with firm confidence said to Ahab, "Go up, eat and drink; for there is the sound of abundance of rain" (1 Kings 18:41). Elijah's ear caught that sound by faith, for no natural sign betokened the imminence of rain.

Now it was time for Elijah to withdraw to the mountaintop, as Christ so often did, and pray. "So Ahab went up to eat and drink. And Elijah went up to the top of Carmel; then he bowed down on the ground, and put his face between his knees" (vs. 42). Self-vindication was not the burden of his prayer but restored favor to Israel, which had so long and habitually slighted God's mercy and gone "awhoring after idols." Elijah prayed for rain. But what lasting benefit would come of rain unless the people were also receptive to the cleansing showers of the Spirit? Who can fathom the depth and intensity of Elijah's prayer? He longed far more for Israel's revival and restoration to godliness than for the renewal of its natural water supplies. But the time had come for both, and in Elijah's prayers the two issues were intertwined.

As one who lived near to God, Elijah felt deeply his own unworthiness. He did not come before the Lord as one who felt empowered to command a blessing, rather he came as a suppliant and intercessor for sinning, apostate Israel, and asked God to signalize His mercy by sending rain. His prayers did not bring an immediate result. Elijah "said to his servant, 'Go up now, look toward the sea.' So he went up and looked, and said, 'There is nothing.' And seven times he said, 'Go again' " (vs. 43).

With characteristically forceful insight Spurgeon comments on this passage:

> "Success is certain when the Lord has promised it. Although you may have pleaded month after month without evidence of answer, it is not possible that the Lord shall be deaf when His people are earnest in a matter which concerns His glory. The prophet on top of Carmel continues to wrestle with God. . . . Six times the servant returned, but on each occa-

sion no word was spoken but 'Go again'. . . . Faith sends expectant hope to look from Carmel's brow, and if nothing is beheld, she sends again and again. So far from being crushed by repeated disappointment, faith is animated to plead more fervently with her God. . . . Delayed answers often send the heart searching itself, and so lead to contrition and spiritual reformation: deadly blows are thus struck at our corruption, and the chambers of imagery are cleansed. The great danger is lest men should faint and miss the blessing.[2]

Important lessons are presented to us in the experience of Elijah. When upon Mt. Carmel he offered the prayer for rain, his faith was tested, but he persevered in making known his request unto God. Six times he prayed earnestly, and yet there was no sign that his petition was granted, but with a strong faith he urged his plea to the throne of grace. Had he given up in discouragement at the sixth time, his prayer would not have been answered, but he persevered till the answer came. We have a God whose ear is not closed to our petitions; and if we prove His word, He will honor our faith. He wants us to have all our interests interwoven with His interests, and then He can safely bless us; for we shall not then take glory to self when the blessing is ours, but shall render all the praise to God. God does not always answer our prayers the first time we call upon Him; for should He do this, we might take it for granted that we had a right to all the favors and blessings bestowed upon us.[3]

This would turn us into spoiled children. We would start treating God like a bellhop-genie, poised to magically carry out all our wishes without delay. Prayer would become a vehicle for attaining our selfish desires. Prayer is a means by which God brings us into harmony with His will, rather than by which He is coaxed to come down to our terms. Real prayer inspires humility and trust in God rather than a demanding self-confidence.

Elijah humbled himself until he was in a condition where

he would not take glory to himself. This is the condition upon which the Lord hears prayer, for then we shall give the praise to Him. . . . He kept reviewing his life to see where he had failed to honor God, he confessed his sins, and thus continued to afflict his soul before God, while watching for a token that his prayer was answered. As he searched his heart, he seemed to be less and less, both in his own estimation and in the sight of God. It seemed to him that he was nothing, and that God was everything; and when he reached the point of renouncing self, while he clung to the Saviour as his only strength and righteousness, the answer came. The servant appeared and said, "Behold, there ariseth a little cloud out of the sea, like a man's hand."[4]

How strikingly Elijah's experience contrasts with that of self-proclaimed reformers who think they wear the prophet's mantle, when God has conferred no such office on them. Their primary work is to pick at flaws in others while remaining insensible to their own sins of pride, peevishness, self-exaltation, and dearth of heaven's grace and love! Theirs is a "ministry" of abrasive denunciation, and that's about all. No fruit of the Spirit, no heartbroken intercession for others, no sacrificial commitment to anyone's salvation is seen in all their labors. Or if these qualities are present, they appear in all too scant a measure. The idealism of these misguided "reformers" is without mercy or true justice. They may be willing to rant in public, but their souls do not weep in secret places for the redemption of souls wandering in sin and darkness. We need to contemplate the example of Elijah, who abased himself on Carmel, praying for his people and for himself that all sin would be washed away in the downpour of God's grace, the rain of His cleansing love and righteousness.

Properly understood, Elijah's example will not inspire us to be fiery fanatics but faithful witnesses and fervent intercessors. Then the work of reformation will go forward in company with repentance and revival, all blending to produce positive and strengthening results. Then we will not be hasty or impatient in our efforts to glorify God. Like Elijah, we will pray earnestly and perseveringly, not to bend God's will to ours but to submerge our will in His and give Him unlimited authority in our lives. This radical transformation takes time and deep attitude change. Prayer provides the opportunity God longs for to give us an entirely new experience that effects a radical new outlook on life. Not a despondent, disgruntled outlook but one that is big with hope, vibrant with love, yet firm in uprightness and integrity. This outlook is illuminated with the Word.

In every Scripture prophecy is seen a promise and in every promise a prophecy of that which shall be when claimed by faith. "From the secret place of prayer came the power that shook the world in the Great Reformation [of the 1500s]. There with holy calmness, the servants of the Lord set their feet upon the rock of His promises."[5] Through such prayerful, enlightened faith, "they subdued kingdoms, wrought righteousness, obtained promises, stopped the mouths of lions, quenched the violence of fire, escaped the edge of the sword, out of weakness were made strong, waxed valiant in fight, turned to flight the armies of aliens. . . . Others were tortured, not accepting deliverance; that they might obtain a better resurrection" (Heb. 11:33-35, KJV).

Elijah's example teaches us that earnest, persistent prayer is vital to serving God effectively. What would you think if someone told you that he had once attempted to put out a brush fire with a bucket of water, and because the fire kept burning, he concluded that water is ineffective in quenching fires? Wouldn't you answer, "You should have kept dousing the fire with water. You might have needed ten buckets or ten thousand gallons, but if you had applied enough water, the fire would have gone out."

Too often we try to deal with the needs and "brush-fire" emergencies of life with unirrigated prayers, and then we pout because nothing special seems to happen; problems continue, or they worsen. Our own internal dryness and unprayerfulness may be a major part of the problem. Through our lack of humility, patience, and kindness, we may throw off sparks that ignite the tinder of troubling circumstances in the drought-stricken lives around us. Then a great conflagration ensues, and like chagrined children we wail "But I prayed and look what happened." Yes, we prayed, a nonsubmissive or halfhearted, two-bucket prayer, expecting God on this account to intervene and make everything change in conformity to our wishes. Such a prayer life has no victories, no maturity, and very little conception of the spiritual issues involved in the science of prayer.

We forget that the primary purpose of prayer is to give God an open road to do what He wants and to make ourselves available as agents for the manifestation of His will in whatever ways He chooses to act. "Seek the Lord with all your heart. Come with zeal, and when you sincerely feel that without the help of God you perish, when you pant after Him as the hart panteth after the water brooks, then the Lord will strengthen you speedily. Then will your peace pass all understanding. If you expect salvation, you must pray. Take time. Be not hurried and careless in your prayers. Beg of God to work in you a thorough reformation, that the fruits of His Spirit may dwell in you, and you shine as lights in the world."[6]

Prayer is not designed to overcome God's reluctance but to take hold of His highest willingness and to give Him unlimited access to our hearts so that He can impart to us His character and guide us according to His will. Prayer is not a password for getting what we want but a passageway for God to take full possession of our hearts—to set up housekeeping there, to make our minds His reception room, our faculties His tools, our homes His workshop, our mouths His message center, our souls His sanctuary. For Elijah all this was a reality. When his servant told him of the small cloud rapidly approaching, Elijah seized on this as sufficient evidence of God's favoring hand. He tarried for no further sign but by faith acted on this token, sending his servant quickly to Ahab with the message, "Prepare your chariot and go down before the rain stops you."

Then came the rain. Not as a languid misty veil, not as a brief cloudburst, but in torrents that swept over the land in undulating waves, curtains of water tumbling in dense folds from the darkened sky. Rain that pelted the earth and drenched everything in minutes; rain that cascaded, saturated, penetrated and cleansed; rain that irrigated the cracked soil and soon called forth its dormant life in luxuriant profusion. Rain that washed away all dusty dryness, removed all thirst, and rinsed away all doubts about the supremacy of Israel's God. Rain that revived, refreshed, and restored.

As Ahab, hoping to escape the coming storm, hastily obeyed Elijah, the inundation broke forth, as from winged clouds releasing the swollen reservoirs of long withheld showers. Elijah ran ahead of the king's chariot, for rain falling in thick gray ropes was all that could be seen. Supernaturally strengthened, Elijah bounded along, guiding the king's chariot safely to the city gates.

> This gracious act of God's messenger shown to a wicked king is a lesson for all who claim to be servants of God, but who are exalted in their own estimation. There are those who feel above performing duties that to them appear menial. They hesitate to perform even needful service, fearing that they will be found doing the work of a servant. These have much to learn from the example of Elijah. By his word the treasures of heaven had been for three years withheld from the earth; he had been signally honored of God, as in answer to his prayer on Carmel, fire had flashed forth from heaven and consumed the sacrifice; his hand had executed the judgment of God in slaying the idolatrous prophets; his petition for rain had been granted. And yet, after the signal triumphs with which God had been pleased to honor his public ministry, he was willing to perform the service of a menial.[7]

Further, in running ahead of the king to guide his chariot to safety, Elijah was signifying his respect for the king's office. Having no thought of thus buying the king's favor, Elijah still honored him as Israel's appointed ruler. In this the prophet shows us how important it is to respect God's duly appointed leaders. We need the humility, faith, prayerfulness, and uncompromising moral courage of Elijah, as well as his loyalty to the church. True reform rules out mutiny against leadership or even silent disregard of its role.

Elijah's treatment of Ahab should also teach leaders how vital it is to be worthy of such respect, as Ahab failed to be. Think how abundantly God's cause would flourish if members and leaders *alike* would pull together in wholehearted obedience to God as colaborers waiting, praying, and working together in anticipation of the golden showers of the latter rain that shall fall bountifully to ripen earth's harvest for the sickle of its coming King!

*Questions for Discussion and Reflection*

1. What connection do you discover between Christ's parable of the importunate widow and Elijah's prayer for rain? Luke 18:1-7.

2. Why was it necessary for Elijah to pray seven times and not just once?

3. Why did Jesus ask the question in Luke 18:8? What relevance does it have for your life?

4. What did the Lord want to "rain" upon His people besides natural water? Hos. 6:3; 10:12.

---

1 The Great Controversy, 525.

2. Charles H. Spurgeon, *Morning and Evening Meditations* (Grand Rapids, Mich.: Zondervan [n.d.]), 545.

3. *Ellen G. White Comments*, SDA Bible Commentary , 7A:96, 97.

4. Ibid., 97.

5. *The Great Controversy*, 210.

6. *Maranatha, 69.*

7. *Prophets and Kings*, 158, 159.

# CHAPTER

# 8

# Elijah's Flight From Fury

lijah led Ahab's chariot through the storm only as far as the city gate. Dashing through the entrance, Ahab wheeled hastily to the shelter of his palace. His day's work now done; Elijah wrapped himself in his mantle and went to sleep by the city wall. Thus ended one of the most significant days in the world's history. The forces of evil had suffered a mighty blow, and truth was signally vindicated. And best of all, many Israelites turned their hearts to God in restored consecration.

But Ahab's account of the day's activity ignited in Jezebel's heart a fire storm of rage. Scorning the clear evidence of God's displeasure with Israel's idolatry and His miraculous confirmation of Elijah's mission, she sent a messenger to inform Elijah that she would have him killed within twenty-four hours. Here Ahab let a golden opportunity slip through his fingers. Instead of overruling his wife's madness, he spinelessly caved in to her rage against the Lord's messenger. He had the authority to banish Baal worship from his kingdom, and every evidence showed that it was God's will for him to do so. But Ahab stands as an archetype of weak government truckling to bigoted religious power that assumes control.

When corrupt religion is more aggressive than corrupt government and the two collaborate, the results are horrendous. The church dominates the state, as it did in medieval Europe, and they combine to become a ruthless engine of destruction acting in the name of God. Their chief victims are the godly. Jezebel stands for corruption in religion taking over the reins of political power. History demonstrates that this arrangement is always disastrous and always poses a special threat to liberty of conscience.

How did Elijah handle Jezebel's announcement of her determination to have him killed? Completely exhausted from the strenuous activities of the day in massively confronting the forces of darkness, he panicked and ran.

> Only a few hours had passed since he had witnessed a wonderful manifestation of divine power, and this should have given assurance that he would not now be forsaken. Had he remained where he was, had he made God his refuge and strength, standing steadfast for the truth, he would have been shielded from harm. The Lord would have given him another signal victory by sending His judgments on Jezebel; and the impression made on the king and the people would have wrought a great reformation.[1]

Although Elijah weakened and fled, we should not be too quick to scorn him for his disappointing reaction. He was a man of like passions as we are, and most of us would probably have done the same thing. We have no room for self-righteousness. How many of us have ever stood as bravely for God's cause as did Elijah? It now seemed to God's prophet that he had no support from anywhere, that he was the sole standing representative of God's truth, with no visible allies. Elijah was a moral hero with a momentary lapse of courage—a lapse that, admittedly, cost the nation dearly. We can learn a lesson from Elijah's crucial moment of faltering—to pray and trust in God at all times, even when appearances look the most forbidding. We can also learn that He will strengthen us to stand at our post of duty even when it looks as though our best efforts for God have yielded disappointing results or have endangered our personal safety.

> Elijah had expected much from the miracle wrought on Carmel. He had hoped that after this display of God's power, Jezebel would no longer have influence over the mind of Ahab, and that there would be a speedy reform throughout Israel. All day on Carmel's height he had toiled without food. Yet when he guided the chariot of Ahab to the gate of Jezreel, his courage was strong, despite the physical strain under which he had labored.

But a reaction such as frequently follows high faith and glorious success was pressing upon Elijah. He feared that the reformation begun on Carmel might not be lasting; and depression seized him.[2]

If Elijah had prayed for God's protection from Jezebel, it would have been granted, and Jezebel's death sentence would have turned upon herself. But temporarily losing his hold on God, Elijah ran for his life through the thick rain in the dark of night. After a night's running with his servant, he stopped at Beersheba. There he left his servant, who must have been puzzled and shaken by his master's hasty flight. Continuing his solitary flight into the wilderness, Elijah at last took shelter beneath a juniper tree. Utterly dejected and weary, he groaned, " 'It is enough; now, O Lord, take away my life; for I am not better than my fathers' " (1 Kings 19:4). Then he fell asleep. What a merciful release from his discouragement and fear!

But God had not abandoned Elijah. An angel stood guard over him, and after allowing him a period of rest, awakened him to eat. How reassuring! Elijah's heaven-sent guardian provided him with freshly baked bread and a bottle of water. Such treatment typifies God's way of supporting us in our discouragements and despair. One night, soon after Jesus' resurrection, as the apostles fruitlessly labored to fish, Christ unexpectedly appeared by the seashore and gave them directions that brought an enormous catch. Then He invited them ashore to eat a hot breakfast He had prepared (see John 21:1-14).

David beautifully captured this aspect of God's gracious dealings with His children: "Thou preparest a table before me in the presence of mine enemies: thou anointest my head with oil; my cup runneth over. Surely goodness and mercy shall follow me all the days of my life . . ." (Ps. 23:5, 6). While we might be tempted to reprove the disheartened or toss a dry slogan their way, instead of giving needed support, God gives them rest and fixes a hot meal, if not with His own hands then by the hands of one of His servants.

When I was a young Bible instructor in Utah and the going was sometimes rough and unproductive, a dear aged saint, Karin Selander, who often assisted me in my work, would invite me to her home and provide me with simple but nourishing and tasty food whose first and most savory ingredient was love. This simple act of compassion and kindness fortified me more than she could ever have realized. It nerved me to press on with my often lonely-seeming task of trying to win souls in a spiritual desert land. Moreover, as slow and hard-won as the results often were, the Lord did grant us fruit for our labors.

So great had been the expenditure of Elijah's energy and so profound his discouragement that after he ate the food offered by the angel, he slept again. Once more the angel allowed him his much needed rest but at the appropriate time awakened him with a touch and said, "Arise and eat, because the journey is too great for you."

He didn't rebuke Elijah and command him to turn back to Samaria. God knew that Elijah needed time to sort through the issues and pray. He needed a renewal of faith under quiet, stress-free conditions. Accordingly, God strengthened His prophet for his continued flight from the wrath of Jezebel, which he really need not have feared at all.

"So he arose, and ate and drank; and he went in the strength of that food forty days and forty nights as far as Horeb, the mount of God." There he found refuge in a cave and felt secure in this rocky, womblike shelter.

God's merciful treatment of Elijah should teach us much about how to deal with others' discouragement. It is not a time for dry moralizing or impassioned utterances on celestial verities, such as Job's friends offered. Rather, it's a time for comforting assurance and affirmation, for tangible deeds of kindness, for hot soup instead of scalding words, for bread instead of blame, for prayer and brotherly affirmation instead of remonstrance and reproof.

When Martin Luther, feeling deserted and alone, walked through the street on his way to a hostile council of inquisitors at Worms, an old soldier darted out from the curious crowd, grasped Luther by the hand, and assured him that Christ would mightily support him in this hour of trial as he stood for the truth. This brief word of reassurance, accompanied by that warm handshake, reinforced Luther at the crucial moment, reviving his courage to stand with lionlike boldness in defense of the gospel before all its enemies.

*Questions for Reflection and Discussion*

1. Elijah was ordinarily a man of dauntless courage. Describe the spiritual and emotional factors that caused his courage to collapse and send him fleeing.

2. What might Elijah have done that would have braced him to stand his ground in the face of Jezebel's threat on his life?

3. Have you ever been so frightened and discouraged by someone's hostility toward you that you fled? How might you have handled the situation differently? How would you handle such a situation today?

4. Outline a plan of action that you intend to follow in helping some discouraged person that you may meet today or in the near future.

---

1. *Prophets and Kings*, 160.

2. Ibid., 160, 161.

# CHAPTER
# 9

# Elijah in Horeb's Cave

**A**s we have seen, if Elijah hadn't run from Jezebel, the reformation he began on Carmel would have opened the way for still greater victories. He might have led Israel into a vigorous and sweeping movement of renewed spiritual life. "Had he waited in faith and patience, God would have shielded His servant and would have given him another signal victory by sending His judgments upon Jezebel."[1] Then the way would have been cleared for a full restoration of pure worship in Israel and a lasting revival and reformation.

But the prophet had new lessons of trust and humility to learn. While the most courageous man in Israel, still Elijah was not flawless. But God didn't abandon him. Instead, He met and reasoned with him at the cave in Horeb. In the history of the world God has never selected people to be prophets because they were completely faultless. True they were "holy men" who spoke under the inspiration of the Holy Spirit (2 Pet. 1:21), but, like everyone else, they had weaknesses to overcome. They were not storybook figures but real people who were also subject to God's counsel and correction. Their character development was not static but constantly progressing toward completeness in Christ.

Elijah was no exception. We should refrain from judging him harshly for his hasty flight from Jezebel. "Those who have not borne weighty responsibilities, or who have not been accustomed to feel very deeply, cannot understand the feelings of Elijah and are not prepared to give him the tender sympathy he deserves. God knows and can read the heart's sore anguish under temptation and sore conflict."[2]

In loving compassion, God permitted Elijah a full night's rest in the "security" of the cave. In the morning He met His weary, dejected servant with the question, "What are you doing here, Elijah?"

This question reverberated with implications. "Three years ago I sent you to King Ahab with a message of judgment. Then I directed you to the brook Cherith where I fed you, and afterward sent you to the widow of Sarepta. I commissioned you to gather king, priests, and people on Carmel that I might vindicate my truth through you. Then I directed you to lead Ahab's chariot back to his palace. But when did I send you to this place? What errand do you have here?"

His voice quivering with bitter anguish, Elijah stated his grievance: "I have been very zealous for the Lord God of hosts; for the children of Israel have forsaken Your covenant, torn down Your altars, and killed Your prophets with the sword. I alone am left; and they seek to take my life" (1 Kings 19:10). Elijah implied by these words that God had placed him, His faithful, devoted servant, in an impossibly difficult situation.

Have you ever been dismayed with God for putting you in circumstances that seemed unreasonably difficult, especially after you strove to carry out His will? If we are unsparingly honest with ourselves, we'll all admit that we've had times of dissatisfaction with God's providences, with events He has allowed in our lives. *"Master, carest Thou not that we perish?"* Every believer is sometimes tempted to feel abandoned by God. But we know in our hearts that God is not in the business of ruining our lives. He wants to set us on the highest vantage ground, and in order to do this, He must sometimes bring us into trying circumstances, "Gennesaret" and "Red Sea" experiences, if you will. He reaches forth His hand of deliverance at the most crucial hour when far more people than ourselves are able to benefit from the manifestation of His providence and power.

When you review your life from this larger perspective, then you won't be so easily perplexed or offended by the crises of your life or the daily difficulties you must meet on the road to the kingdom.[3] You will take courage from God's counsel to Joshua. "Have I not commanded you? Be strong and of good courage; do not be afraid, nor be dismayed, for the Lord your God is with you wherever you go" (Josh. 1:9). If we abide in God's Word and fellowship, this promise will unfold with endless power and variety of application in our daily lives.

But Elijah had temporarily lost sight of this promise, which he must have known and cherished. God skillfully brought him out of his querulous despondency. Instead of refuting Elijah's complaint, He gave him a series of object lessons. He said, "Go out and stand on the mountain before the Lord" (1 Kings 19:11). This is good advice for us all in times of discouragement and mourning over our own frailties and failures. Rather than cower in the cave of despair, let us step into the light and ascend Mount Zion on whose top we are summoned to stand triumphantly with Jesus (Heb. 12:22-24; Rev. 14:1).

Positioning himself as directed, Elijah waited. Then the Lord passed by, and a wind of such force sprang up that it tore boulders from the mountain and split the rocks. But the Lord was not in the wind. Then an earthquake shook the mountain and surrounding area, but the Lord was not in the earthquake. Next, a fire rolled across the desert terrain, but the Lord was not in the fire.

"'And after the fire a still small voice. So it was, when Elijah heard it, that he wrapped his face in his mantle and went out, and stood in the entrance of the cave'" (1 Kings 19:12, 13). God then repeated His question, "'What are you doing here, Elijah?'" Elijah returned the same answer as before, only this time he was far more chastened in outlook. His accusing tone melted away, replaced with humility, submission, and renewed openness to God's direction.

It is not always the dramatic incidents and lofty speeches that make the most profound impression on our hearts. Christ speaking to us from the cross, from the mercy seat, and by the sweet influences of His Holy Spirit has the deepest effect in transforming and developing our character and moving us to noble action. This still small voice of the Spirit is willing to constantly guide us in harmony with Scripture. "Your ears shall hear a word behind you, saying, 'This is the way, walk in it,' whenever you turn to the right hand or whenever you turn to the left" (Isa. 30:21).

We can discern from Elijah's experience on Horeb some additional lessons of great importance for us today. First, consider what Elijah had witnessed on Carmel. God did not permit Satan to work a miracle on behalf of the cavorting priests of Baal. Their most frantic efforts to conjure up rain were futile. But in these last days the modern "priests of Baal," Satan's deluded religious agents, will be able to work with "all power, signs, and lying wonders." "For false christs and false prophets will arise and show great signs and wonders, so as to deceive, if possible, even the elect" (2 Thess. 2:9; Matt. 24:24).

Elijah's experience on Horeb presents a memorable safeguard against placing hasty confidence in miracles, signs, and wonders, and making them the primary criteria of our faith.[4] One word of truth from Scripture is more authoritative than the mightiest display of miracles. Our reliance must not be in the power of miracles, or in worship exercises full of high-voltage animation, but in the authority of God's Word, which speaks to us from Scripture, far more often in a still small voice than in thunder tones. This flies in the face of modern religion's own "big-bang" theory, which suggests that the louder the music, the more strident the preaching, and the more sensational the activities, the greater is the converting effect. This is a fallacy.

Receptiveness to God's voice is the greatest blessing we could seek. Such keen sensitivity is illustrated by the way Thomas Edison invented the phonograph. While he was singing into the mouthpiece of a telephone to test its acoustic capabilities, a fine steel point responding to the vibrations rose from the transmitter field, slightly pricking his finger. This sparked Edison's dream of recording the human voice by tracking a sound-activated needle over a delicate but durable surface. Edison might have passed off the needle-prick as an extraneous incident, a minor annoyance. But his mind was constantly attuned to the possibility of new inventions for the betterment of humankind.

Likewise, God's still small voice often speaks to us in seemingly casual, insignificant ways. Yet to a mind constantly reaching out for God, His voice and promptings will become increasingly distinct. Those whose hearts pant for God's presence and fellowship will not need miracles or marvels to discern His leading and purpose.

Elijah had been confronted with such an intense display of dramatic and sensational events on Carmel that he needed a restored sensitivity to God's presence and leading. God took the most rehabilitative course possible on Elijah's behalf. Instead of dismissing him from duty, He gave him some new tasks to perform. He told Elijah to "anoint three,"—Hazael as king over Syria, Jehu as king over Israel, and Elisha as Elijah's own successor.[5]

Then the Lord added a startling disclosure—"I have yet 7,000 in Israel who have not bowed the knee to Baal." In a way, this last statement, which seemed to come almost as an afterthought, was the most important. Elijah was not God's sole representative! The Lord had 7,000 faithful worshipers in Israel. Elisha and his family were among that number. And so it is in this world of spiritual darkness and seemingly unchecked apostasy. God has His firmament of faithful ones. Some are doing an open work in public, others He holds in reserve until His appointed time.

According to Revelation 14, God has 144,000 in these last days whose loyalty to Him is unshakable. I have no burden to discuss whether this number is literal or figurative. One thing is certain, these 144,000 are God's messengers to help enlighten the world with His everlasting gospel, and their labors shall bring a humanly uncountable harvest of converts to Christ and His kingdom (Rev. 7:1-14; 14:1-16). Meanwhile, we are not to number Israel or pass judgment on the church for its seeming lack of Elijahs. We should each resolve to be as true to God and His cause as Elijah was but avoid Elijah's mistake of seeing himself as God's only loyal witness or as one of His very few.

Elijah's history offers us vastly more than good Bible stories for children or a few rousing Sabbath sermons. It pulsates with significance for our time. The parallels between the religious crises in Elijah's day and ours are emphatic and momentous. Moreover, we have much to learn from Elijah's interaction with God, who strengthened His servant to courageously persevere as His witness in the face of enormous opposition and personal risk.

We should keep in mind that because Elijah's heart was moved with compassion to see so many living in spiritual darkness and destitution, God called him to special service as His messenger. As he faithfully carried out his commission, Elijah discovered the cost of discipleship. His faltering over the danger confronting him did not mean he was faithless or fickle.

Despondency may shake the most heroic faith and weaken the most steadfast will. But God understands, and He still pities and loves. He reads the motives and purposes of the heart. To wait patiently, to trust when everything looks dark, is the lesson that the leaders of God's work need to learn. Heaven will not fail them in their day of adversity. Nothing is apparently more helpless, yet really more invincible, than the soul that feels its own nothingness and relies wholly on God.

Not alone for men in positions of large responsibility is the lesson of Elijah's experience in learning anew how to trust God in the hour of trial. He who was Elijah's strength is strong to uphold every struggling child of His, no matter how weak. Of everyone He expects loyalty, and to everyone He grants power according to the need. In his own strength man is strengthless; but in the might of God he may be strong to overcome evil and to help others to overcome. . . .

Abiding in God's love, you may stand every test. The righteousness of Christ alone can give you power to stem the tide of evil that is sweeping over the world. Bring faith into your experience. Faith lightens every burden, relieves every weariness.[6]

As we faithfully serve God, He will make His cause triumph through us. "Thanks be to God who gives us the victory through our Lord Jesus Christ" (1 Cor. 15:57).

From the standpoint of high drama, the pinnacle of Elijah's story was the great reformation he launched on Carmel, but the remaining incidents of his life are full of enduring significance. We will look at these incidents in the next couple of chapters.

*Questions for Discussion and Reflection*

1. Why did God send the wind, earthquake, and fire before He spoke to Elijah with a still, small voice? What lessons can we learn from this today?

2. What spiritual influence on society do you think the 7,000 exerted who had not bowed the knee to Baal? Why were they unknown to Elijah?

3. What promises in God's Word are especially meaningful to you when you face times of testing and trial for your faith?

4. Why didn't God deal more sternly with Elijah for fleeing from Jezebel? After Elijah had failed Him, why did God give him additional important services to perform? How should we deal with the faithful who falter?

---

1. *Testimonies for the Church*, 3:290.

2. Ibid., 291.

3. Consider Paul's outlook of the trials and tragedies of his life: 1 Cor. 4:9-14; 2 Cor. 1:3-6; 2:14-17; 4:6-18. May we embrace this large and enlightened view of life's sufferings and sorrows!

4. For further light on this important subject, see the chapter "Miracles Not a Test of God's Favor," in *Selected Messages*, 2:48-55.

5. Hazael, heathen king of Syria, was God's punishing rod sent to chasten His rebellious people, much as did Nebuchadnezzar several generations later. And Jehu was a model of what every true reformer is not—hasty, hotheaded, and violent. As Israel's king he uprooted most idolatry from the land but not with love. His administration brought a purge of Baal worship but not a revival of true godliness. Moreover, he did

not put a stop to the worship of golden calves instituted by Jeroboam, Israel's first king. He ordered the death of Jezebel and all of Ahab's sons but only to clear the way for his absolute rule over Israel. Scripture leaves this grim record of Jehu: "But Jehu took no heed to walk in the law of the Lord God of Israel with all his heart; for he did not depart from the sins of Jeroboam, who had made Israel sin" (2 Kings 10:31).

6. *Prophets and Kings*, 174, 175.

# CHAPTER
# 10

# Elijah, Friend of Humanity

Have you ever wondered why Scripture is so full of narrative incident and biographical detail? After all, the Bible, as God's inspired book, reveals the bedrock truths of life. No other record or resource defines right and wrong with such authority. We might wonder then, "Why doesn't God spell out all doctrine in a systematic fashion and give us the one, two, threes and A, B, Cs of moral instruction, the way a college textbook would?" It would seem sure to make the theory of truth easier to grasp than by having it scattered, as it is, throughout the Bible. Or would it?

Would sound doctrine gain wider acceptance and deeper appreciation if Scripture presented it as a series of formal propositions, like Euclidean geometry? Probably not. Bible doctrine is more than a formulation and codifying of pure morals; it describes the infrastructure of real life, life as God means it to be. Bible doctrine is the portrayal of heaven's redeeming interaction with earth.

God wants us to understand not sound doctrine only but also its *practical application*, which includes right principles of action and personal relationship. Rather than by abstract statement, these principles are best taught through example and illustration. Elijah's history is a good example of God's method of teaching fundamental truths combined with character-building lessons.

In sending Elijah, God had more in mind than the restoration of pure doctrine in Israel; He wanted to reclaim their hearts and affections. True, Elijah was a great reformer, and man of unswerving loyalty to principle. Others have also been like this, but some of them have been cold and unfeeling—moral icebergs. Such a man Elijah was not. Scripture provides us with fascinating sidelights on Elijah as a person, sidelights that reveal his profound humanness combined with lionlike moral courage. Moreover, these sidelights reveal God's desire to compassionately bring restoration to His people, a restoration that He mediates in large part through His earthly servants.

Consider again Elijah's kindness to the God-fearing widow of Sarepta. He used his supernatural authority not just to declare a drought upon Israel but to secure for the poverty-stricken widow a bountiful supply of grain and oil during this period of general dearth. He acted also as the Lord's intermediary in restoring her son to life. Plainly, Elijah was not detached and indifferent to the needs of others. He wasn't so wound up with his message that he forgot to care about people and their special needs.

Nor were his religious reforms of a cold, unfeeling nature. On Carmel he prayed that God would turn the *hearts* of the people back to Himself. Elijah wasn't intent on bringing about moral renovation merely; he longed for the people to have renewed love for their Creator and Provider. This approach to reform bears no pungent reek of legalism, no repellent glare of Pharisaism. Further, Elijah's sevenfold prayer for rain upon Israel proves his longing for prosperity to return to the nation. He didn't pray, "Lord, give them three months' probation, and if the spirit of reform continues, then cautiously send them a little rain to confirm your provisional acceptance of them. See how it goes with the people, and if they are appreciative and obedient, then send them a little more rain, and so continue the process until You are sure of their loyalty."

No sooner had the people on Mount Carmel confessed their belief in Yahweh and renounced Baal worship than Elijah prayed for rain. And God sent rain in abundance, just as Elijah had desired and anticipated He would.

Then after his flight to Horeb and return to his labors for Israel,

Elijah dealt as a noble advocate of social justice. When Ahab, through connivance at his wife's evil plot, killed Naboth and confiscated his vineyard, Elijah reproved the king for his dastardly deed. We see that God's reformer didn't reserve his efforts merely for large issues that would gain publicity but at his own risk served as a vindicator of the oppressed (see 1 Kings 21). Elijah boldly confronted the weak but mean-spirited king with God's sentence upon him for violating the laws of respect for individual life and property. No mere ideologue would do this, but only a true champion of human rights.

Then we think of Elijah's latter-day work leading up to his translation. Longing to see the progressive work of reform continue after his departure, he reestablished the schools of the prophets, which had ceased operation during Jezebel's raging warfare against Israel's God. But despite her deadly opposition, 7,000 had not bowed the knee to Baal. Many who composed this number must have filled the ranks of these revived schools.

As a wise undershepherd, Elijah and his successor in training, Elisha, toured these schools to instruct and encourage their students, whose lives were committed to the advancement of reform and the maintenance of Israel's election as God's covenant-keeping people. To these brave missionaries Elijah was a father and a reforming hero. What impetus and courage he must have given to their labors! They knew that Elijah felt and lived the truths he preached and that was the secret of his influence.

Without these biographical details, we might very easily imagine Elijah in a distorted light that detracts from the power of his great ministry. We might perceive him as a kind of incarnate thunderbolt that struck fiercely at evil but had no more personality or human warmth than Mount Everest. However, Elijah's intense commitment to the rights and needs of humanity and to the welfare of God's people imparts a mellow glow of meaning to the prophecy that God's future Elijahs would "turn the hearts of the fathers to the children, and the hearts of the children to their fathers" (Mal. 4:6).

Few are such incorruptible defenders of honor and justice as was the rugged prophet of Gilead (1 Kings 17:1). Fewer still are the people of profound compassion who unite prophetic vision with such effectual deeds of kindness as did this bold messenger of the rocky wilderness. For Gilead was more than a place of craggy landscape and rustic nomads; it was also the source of a royal balm for the cure of deep inner wounds; metaphorically, it is the place from which the Great Physician comes forth to heal the "sin-sick soul." Lord, send us Elijahs today who will bring Your balm of healing, as well as the celestial fires of purification!

*Questions for Discussion and Reflection*

1. Consider Isaiah 28:9, 10. Why do you think God has seen fit to present doctrinal teaching in the framework of scriptural history and biography?

2. Why should we be careful not to separate a systematic knowledge of Bible doctrine from the historical and biographical portions of Scripture, and vice versa?

3. We have seen that Elijah was a man of compassion, faith, and social justice. What kinds of issues should God's modern-day Elijahs be concerned about? At the same time, how can we avoid the danger of falling into an issues-centered "social gospel"?

4. If a person is doctrinally right about everything but not very concerned about the personal welfare of others, how would that affect his influence as a witness for Christ?

# CHAPTER
# 11

# Elijah's Final Work and Translation

**O**n Horeb God instructed Elijah to anoint another prophet in his place, Elisha, the son of Shaphat, in Abelmehola, situated in the fertile valley of Jordan. This was the most important part of Elijah's remaining commission, for Elisha was to carry on the mighty work of reform begun on Carmel. Elisha was from a family comprising part of Israel's 7,000 who had not bowed the knee to Baal. "Theirs was a home where God was honored and where allegiance to the faith of ancient Israel was the rule of daily life."[1]

Elisha means "salvation of God." Even more than that of Elijah, Elisha's mission was to emphasize God's salvation, without any diminution of His holy requirements. Together he and his teacher visited the schools of the prophets, which Elijah had revitalized. The object of their joint labors was to restore Israel to a knowledge of God through the teaching and personal example of those who attended these schools.

God wanted Israel to preserve its distinctive character as His chosen people, so that they might be light-bearers to the world and point all to the universally offered salvation of the coming Messiah. He sought to diffusively convey the principles of His truth through the avenue of education rather than by startling miracles to jolt the people from complacency and ignorance. In our time also, Christian education plays a central role in keeping the mission of God's church alive.

The most essential education for today's youth, and that which will fit them for the higher grades of the school above, is an education that will teach them how to reveal the will of God to the world.

Just before Elijah was taken to heaven, he visited the schools of the prophets, and instructed the students on the most important points of their education. The lessons he had given them on former visits, he now repeated, impressing upon the minds of the youth the importance of letting simplicity mark every feature of their education. Only in this way could they receive the mold of heaven, and go forth to work in the ways of the Lord. If conducted as God designs they should be, our schools in these closing days of the message will do a similar work to that done by the schools of the prophets.[2]

God purposed to extend the great work Elijah had begun, and these schools dedicated to the teaching of Scripture, prayer, and sacred history, music, and poetry, combined with manual training, were the perfect vehicle for perpetuating the knowledge of God's ways. Graduates from these schools could support themselves anywhere as they mingled with society to instruct receptive minds and serve as models of consecrated living. They were to operate not as consumers but as contributors to the general welfare of Israel. After Elijah's departure, Elisha was to have the oversight of this important work that penetrated Hebrew society like a preserving salt.

At first Elisha's duties for Elijah were small and seemingly insignificant. It looked as though he was called to be little more than an attendant to pour water on Elijah's hands and perform other menial services (see 2 Kings 3:11). But through these commonplace duties he learned lessons of humility and service. His regular daily contact with the older prophet was a university education in itself.

For several years after the call of Elisha, Elijah and Elisha labored together, the younger man daily gaining greater pre-paredness for his work. Elijah had been God's instrument for the overthrow of gigantic evils. The idolatry which, sup-ported by Ahab and the heathen Jezebel, had seduced the nation, had been given a decided check. Baal's prophets had been slain. The whole people of Israel had been deeply stirred, and many were returning to the worship of God. As Elijah's successor, Elisha, by careful, patient instruction, must endeavor to guide Israel in safe paths. His association with Elijah, the greatest prophet since the days of Moses, prepared him for the work that he was soon to take up alone.[3]

Shortly before Elijah's translation, he and Elisha briefly visited the schools of the prophets in Gilgal, Jericho, and Bethel (2 Kings 2:1-7). God had revealed to the prophets at these schools that He would take Elijah from them. Evidently God wished to give promi-nence to this event. Not only would He thus signalize the honor in which He held the reformer-prophet but would also accentuate Elisha's appointment as Elijah's legitimate successor.

By keeping Elijah itinerant, the Lord had other purposes in mind as well. "When He was preparing Elijah for translation, [God] moved him from place to place that he might not settle down at ease, and thus fail of obtaining spiritual power. And it was God's design that Elijah's influence should be a power to help many souls to gain a wider, more helpful experience."[4]

Knowing that his time on earth was drawing to a close, Elijah asked Elisha to stay behind at each of the schools they visited. But Elisha would not leave his mentor's side. His devotion to him was too great. He did not wish to miss any part of the blessing God might minister to him through Elijah. He followed him as de-votedly as we should all follow Christ, whom Elijah represented.

Before his ascension to glory, Elijah asked his young protégé a significant question: "Ask what I shall do for thee before I am taken away from thee." Unhesitatingly Elisha replied, "I pray thee, let a double portion of thy spirit be upon me" (2 Kings 2:9, KJV).

Elisha knew that without the Spirit of God, a person's work is powerless and void. Recognizing his call as Elijah's successor, Elisha wanted to be filled with the Spirit that gave power and authority to Elijah's work. His request was in accordance with the instruction in Deuteronomy 21:17, that the elder son was to receive twofold the inheritance of the younger.

Thus Elisha was not asking for a twofold measure of Elijah's power but for a firstborn son's inheritance; that is, for a continuation of the same spiritual grace that was upon Elijah. In this way only could he perform service that was as far-reaching and effective as Israel needed in coming days. His request was not vain or self-exalting. Elisha humbly realized his utter dependence upon God and need for His indwelling presence and power.

But he asked no light thing. To be in the front lines of God's service is an enormous challenge. One goes forth as a warrior for the Lord. Numerous are the battles, subtle and potent the conflicts, endless the challenges, as the march of the gospel progresses toward Armageddon and the final overthrow of all evil. But God's power and wisdom is equal to it all, and He is the sufficiency of all His servants who wholly rely on Him.

Elijah replied, "You have asked a hard thing. Nevertheless if you see me when I am taken from you, it shall be so for you, but if not, it shall not be so" (2 Kings 2:10).

This exchange took place at the river Jordan, where ancient Israel had crossed into the Promised Land, and where John the Baptist, eight centuries later, would baptize people in preparation for their pilgrimage to the heavenly Canaan.

But now the hour of Elijah's coronation and exaltation had come. "Then it happened as they continued on and talked, that suddenly a chariot of fire appeared with horses of fire, and separated the two of them; and Elijah went up by a whirlwind into heaven" (vs. 11).

His heart bursting with anguish and awe-struck appreciation, Elisha exclaimed on witnessing this glorious scene, "My father, my father, the chariot of Israel and the horsemen thereof!" Elijah's translation vindicated his message and mission. Heaven's estimate of him was higher than that of men. Elisha understood that his master had been as a chariot to Israel and the horsemen thereof, for he had single-handedly conquered the hosts of apostasy that were oppressing the nation and keeping it in spiritual darkness.

Except for the time of his flight from Jezebel, the Lord had held the reins of Elijah's life, making it a vehicle for the performance of His will. Elijah had been the burning lantern that guided the nation back to God and true worship. How fitting was the honor that the Lord bestowed on him for his valiant service.

As suddenly as he had burst onto the stage of action in Scripture, just so suddenly did he disappear. Emerging from obscurity to serve and magnify God, he is promoted to infinite honor in a blazing flash of glory—translated without seeing death. No critic of his could nullify that honor or detract from its glory.

> Elijah was a type of the saints who will be living on the earth at the time of the second advent of Christ and who will be "changed in a moment, in the twinkling of an eye, at the last trump," without tasting of death. 1 Corinthians 15:51, 52. It was as a representative of those who shall be thus translated that Elijah, near the close of Christ's earthly ministry, was permitted to stand with Moses by the side of the Saviour on the mount of transfiguration.[5]

There it was Elijah's privilege to speak to Jesus of the atoning sacrifice He was to accomplish at Jerusalem. How fitting that this prophet whose whole life was dedicated to the restoration of pure worship that exalts the Messiah should be appointed for the sublime errand of encouraging his Redeemer to consummate the plan of the ages by which all may be saved who say Yes to Jesus and the fullness of His redemption. Consider Elijah as the friend of the Messiah and honored champion of His cause, and you will see many gospel lessons radiating from the life of this prophet of fire!

*Questions for Discussion and Reflection*

1. Think of a situation in which God replaced with a successor some spiritual leader whom you greatly admired. Comment on how

the contrasting talents of that successor gave special continuity and expansion to God's work.

2. What was the special value of the schools of the prophets that Elijah reestablished? How does Christian education today compare with and differ from the work and curriculum of these schools?

3. What does Elijah's translation without tasting death reveal about God's appraisal of Elijah? Why did He select him for this special honor?

4. Read 2 Kings 2:12-15. What significance do you see in Elisha's tearing his own clothes in two pieces. What significance do you see in the parting of the Jordan when Elisha struck the river with Elijah's mantle?

---

1. *Prophets and Kings*, 217.

2. *Fundamentals of Christian Education*, 512. For more information on the schools of the prophets, see entry entitled "Schools, Hebrew," section 3, in *Unger's Bible Dictionary* and *Patriarchs and Prophets*, 592-602, chapter entitled "The Schools of the Prophets." *Testimonies for the Church*, 6:126-167 sets forth valuable counsel on how to conduct our educational work on the highest plane of reform so that we can operate schools that mirror the work and influence of the schools of the prophets. Today we are "prisoners of hope" *(Testimonies for the Church*, 6:145). May we as a people heed God's counsel in its fullest and finest bearings!

3. *Prophets and Kings*, 224.

4. *Ellen G. White Comments*, *SDA Bible Commentary*, 7A:98.

5. *Prophets and Kings*, 227.

# CHAPTER
# 12

# Elijah and Elisha Contrasted

We have looked in considerable detail at the work of Elijah. His difficult mission demanded moral stamina in defense of truth for God's honor and his country's redemption. Israel's apostasy was so flagrant and firmly entrenched in Elijah's day that had he been a mild, soft-spoken man, his message and reformatory mission would have been entirely ignored. God needed to send a man of dauntless courage and soldierly fortitude to stand for His cause. Elijah was just such a man, although he was never needlessly stern or forceful in his treatment of anyone. Rather, as we have seen, he was kind and compassionate. To the repentant and to those who were afflicted by injustice, his words "were as the Balm of Gilead."

Martin Luther, facing similar circumstances in Christendom, was a man of Elijah-like stamina and valor for truth. He didn't flinch from his arduous task of stern reform. But he was also a tender-hearted man, generous, kind, forgiving, and hospitable. Being studious and reflective, Luther would rather have been a scholar and preacher than an overturner of a hopelessly corrupt ecclesiastical system. Yet God endowed him with a toughness and tenacity that suited him for this thankless but infinitely necessary role.[1]

Christian life is more than many take it to be. It does not

consist wholly in gentleness, patience, meekness, and kind-liness. These graces are essential; but there is need also of courage, force, energy, and perseverance. The path that Christ marks out is a narrow, self-denying path. To enter that path and press on through difficulties and discourage-ments requires men who are more than weaklings.[2]

People of energy, drive, and determination are needed in God's work today. People to whom moral compromise is profoundly ab-horrent and who will do exploits to uphold the honor of God and extricate souls from the entangling darkness of apostasy and sin. Although people like Elijah are vitally needed today, it would be a mistake to suppose that all of God's faithful servants must be like Elijah in assertiveness and militant zeal. We do not all fit into the same mold.

Elijah had a very special ministry, a divinely appointed commis-sion, and along with that commission he had character qualifica-tions that enabled him to carry it out successfully. As Israel's great-est reformer, his was also a ministry of reconciliation. Many today who deeply and honestly recognize the need for reform in our church have somehow gotten a wrong idea of Elijah's personality and mission. They know that the church needs Elijahs today.[3] But they translate this recognition into harsh, condemnatory words and actions. Consider this perceptive passage from Ellen White:

Some with the best of motives, and possessing capabili-ties for great usefulness, utterly fail in times of trial in the church, for want of the love and mercy that dwelt so richly in the heart of Christ. They see one in error; and instead of helping him they hold themselves aloof. They are inclined to make unpleasant allusions, and to touch sensitive spots when they might avoid them. Self comes up and bears sway, and they give pain and stir up wrong feelings. However pure their intentions, their efforts to do good nearly always re-sult in failure, if not in actual harm, because the tenderness and compassion of Christ are wanting. They would make very good surgeons, but they are very poor nurses. They have not the tact that is born of love. If they had this, they would know how to speak the right word and do the right thing at the right time and in the right place. Others may have no more sincere desires to do right, no deeper interest in the cause of God; they may be no more true and loyal, their sympathies no deeper, their love no warmer; yet because of their gentleness and tact they are far more successful in winning back the erring.[4]

This passage is worth pondering in detail. Let's look at it analytically.

1. It recognizes that the church has conscientious souls zealous for the right but lacking in grace to be effective reformers.

2.It recognizes that the church has trials, problems, and serious imperfections. And it does not say that these problems should be left unaddressed and unremedied.

3. It points out that some who detect errors in their brethren, instead of drawing helpfully near, "hold themselves aloof." Taken to its extreme, this can result in a spirit of separatism and independence in some concerned observers who note the multiplicity of problems that actually exist in the church. It can also result in being a constant critic of others, a chronic faultfinder. One can thereby end up being a judgmental critic of administrators, pastors, and officers of the church, thus filling the ears of church members with a running commentary on the real and supposed evils in the church and the perceived inadequacy of its leaders. What can this result in but alienation, division, and discouragement, all engendered in the name of morality and reform?

4. It states that some of these well-intentioned persons "make unpleasant allusions" and "touch sensitive spots," bringing up sensitive issues without God's direction. Without their realizing it, "self" takes the throne in their reformatory efforts, and they fail to exhibit the restoring love of Christ and the healing power of His grace.

5. "However pure their intentions," they inflict needless pain on those they are trying to correct and thus injure the cause of reform. They lack "the tenderness and compassion of Christ."

6. They know how to administer wounds, but they don't know

how to bind them up, hence the characterization "good surgeons" but "poor nurses." They have little concept of how to be nurturing and comforting. "Corrector of heretics, defender of the faith" is their armor-clad mission, but alas, they end up doing neither task effectively.

7. Now, here's the most thought-provoking part—others who are no more (and no less) sincere and committed to truth, and no deeper in sympathy than are militant reformers, accomplish far more to win back the erring, simply because in their efforts to do so they are gentle and tactful.

This passage points to some practical implications for us as a church today. For example, church leaders and regular members need to be better able to recognize the sincerity and commitment of many who are abrasive in their efforts at reform. My observation is that as a church, we have sometimes been too hasty in writing off tactless critics as dangerous people. We have not always respectfully acknowledged that they are as sincere and fervent for truth as we ought to be. Sometimes we have been too defensive. Determined to expose the dangerous tendencies of excessively militant reform, we often have failed to humbly acknowledge, as did Israel's prophets of old, that "we have sinned and wrought great provocations in Israel."

A stonewalling disinclination to honestly and openly admit our failings, or corporate backslidings and deficiencies, has provoked some of our extreme critics to become ever more strident in their denunciations of the church. And because they have documented evidence to prove at least *some* of their critical views, they have a following among some of our own believers who retain membership in the organized church but are torn between the militant independents and the organized body.

I don't wish to imply that the church should be bullied about by smoking firebrands who are implacably opposed to the organized church and fiercely loyal to their own bank accounts filled with the tithes and offerings of their admirers. This species of extremists has always existed and will continue to exist until the close of time. We need to pray that God will give our members spiritual discernment not to fall into the clutches of those who equate reform with perpetual divisiveness and scandal-mongering. I have been astonished and agonized to see some church members who appear rational become spellbound by videotapes and literature that emit a spirit of triumphalism in exposing the most shameful scandals that can be detected (see Prov. 12:18; 16:24; 18:8). And need I say that the reports brought forth are often unfactual or else present such a distortion of the facts as to be indistinguishable from falsehood.

Nevertheless, I feel that we as a church should acknowledge more openly than we do the deep need for repentance and revival. Not that reference to these matters is altogether lacking in our preaching and publications. But we could well afford to make progress in this line. The net result will not be the destruction of the church but a strengthening of it in purity, love, service, and unity. After all, our greatest and most urgent need as a people is a revival of true godliness.[5] In echoing this statement, however, I want always to remember (and I hope every reader will join me in this desire) that *I* need revival and reformation, *I* need to humble *my* heart in the dust, *I* need to plead with God to cleanse *me* of all sin and imbue *me* with His grace.

I can flail away at the real or imaginary faults in the church all day long, but unless my soul is growing in Christlikeness, I would be deluded to think of myself as an anointed reformer like Elijah or Martin Luther. At best, I would simply be a dwarfed caricature of these noble reformers, and at worst a twisted, tormented counterfeit, a whirling dervish who slices off every ear within reach of my scorpion-shaped scimitar, which I would call God's word wielded with noble courage and directness. To do this would be to confuse assault with reform and hostility with zeal for God's glory. Reformers, yes—let us embrace the call with humility, courage, and love. Ravagers, no—let us relinquish all rudeness, rashness and animosity in the work we attempt for God.

"Of all people in the world reformers should be the most unselfish, the most kind, the most courteous. In their lives should be seen the true goodness of unselfish deeds."[6]

Such a man was Elisha. And that is why no study of reform, especially in the context of Elijah's message and mission, is balanced without giving consideration to Elisha, whom God appointed to continue the reform that Elijah began.

In every age, the call of the hour is answered by the coming of the man. The Lord is gracious. He understands the
situation. His will today is that for the present time the lamb-
like kindness of Elisha shall exceed the severity of Elijah. . . .

Whether the present work be to break down or to build
up, to reinstate the old or to give place to the new, to
enforce the demands of equity and judgment or to encourage hope and courage, and faith, the Lord knows what
is needed. He is looking on. He, the great Master worker,
is sure to have the very man for the place ready to do the
work, when those connected with the work are ready for
the change. . . .

He who wears the mantle, not of Elijah, but of Christ, will
give evidence that he keeps his eye fixed on the Saviour.
Imbued with Christ's Spirit, he is fitted to teach. He is constantly under the influences of the high and holy impressions made by God.

Elisha received a double portion of the spirit that had
rested on Elijah. In him the power of Elijah's spirit was united
with the gentleness, mercy, and tender compassion of the
spirit of Christ.[7]

The work of Elisha as a prophet was in some respects
very different from that of Elijah. To Elijah had been committed messages of condemnation and judgment; his was
the voice of fearless reproof, calling king and people to turn
from their evil ways. Elisha's was a more peaceful mission;
his it was to build up and strengthen the work that Elijah
had begun; to teach the people the way of the Lord. Inspiration pictures him as coming into personal touch with the
people, surrounded by the sons of the prophets, bringing by
his miracles and his ministry healing and rejoicing.[8]

Elisha's history helps us recognize that heaven's work and purposes are not static. God did not appoint Elisha to be a second-class imitation of Elijah but to extend his work of reform with the addition of personal qualities that were not so prominently featured (though not absent) in his mentor—tenderness, patience, tact. We should be reluctant to criticize the way others do their work for the Lord. In some people we might wish to see more fire and flash; in others we might wish these elements were less active. But we need to give each of God's servants latitude to be what He made them and not try to refashion anyone into our image of the "ideal."

In the strength of the Lord Elisha accomplished extraordinary things. Beginning as a lowly servant of Elijah, to pour water on his hands (2 Kings 3:11), his responsibilities progressed in depth and complexity. Following Elijah's translation, He presided over the schools of the prophets and was instrumental in working more miracles than any other Old Testament prophet. His courage, integrity, compassion, and quiet strength made him a wonder in Israel and served to magnify the Lord's name and word in all neighboring Gentile kingdoms. He exemplified the value of a life devoted wholeheartedly to the advancement of God's kingdom and the glory of His name.

In character, vision, and consecration, Elisha's later counterparts are people like William Carey, William Miller, Booker T. Washington, and W. D. Frazee—unobtrusive people who labored nobly for the Lord without fanfare but with great effect. Diplomatic but resolute, they plowed on steadily with their divinely appointed mission; and though never widely popular, they achieved much in their respective spheres of service for Christ because, like John the Baptist, the guiding credo of their lives was "He must increase, but I must decrease."

## Questions for Discussion and Reflection

1. If great social reformers like Frederick Douglass, Henry Ward Beecher, and other Abolitionists had not existed, how and when do you think slavery would have ended in the United States?

2. If ancient Israel and the Christian church had never had any

reformers, how would that lack have affected the history of the human race?

3. What qualities do you admire in a reformer? What qualities or traits could harm the influence of a would-be reformer?

4. Contrast Elisha with Elijah. What qualities do you see in Elisha that were not so evident in his master? Why were both men needed to forward the work of reform? Read 2 Kings 2:23-25. Why did Elisha's ministry after Elijah's translation begin on such a stern note? Why wasn't it necessary for Elisha's ministry to continue that way? See *Prophets and Kings*, 235-237.

---

1. In reference to the valiant ministry of John Penry, a young English reformer, his biographer wrote: "In common with all martyrs and reformers he had strong convictions, and in the expression of them, he employed terms that are felt to be too startling and vehement in an age of compromise. Yet, like Wycliffe, Latimer, and Luther, he had a reason for his moral severity, and the effect was beneficial. The work of the pioneer differs from that of the peaceful cultivator who follows in his track. Let us not while we sit beneath the shade of the real tree of liberty, rooted by the storm of persecution and watered by the blood of the martyrs, blame them, that in planting it, and in effecting a clearance for us, they were wanting in some of the graces of manner on which we pride ourselves. We may become effeminate in our love of refinement and lose the great inheritance entrusted to us" (John Waddington, *Penry the Pilgrim Martyr* [London, 1854], 205).

We know from the apocalyptic visions of John that the liberties we now enjoy will soon be abrogated worldwide. But fortunately, God's last-day witnesses, while called on to be firm and resolute for the truth, have no calling or authorization to be belligerent or vituperative in its defense.

2. *Ministry of Healing*, 497.

3. *Gospel Workers,* 150; *Prophets and Kings,* 142.

4. *Testimonies for the Church*, 5:349, 350.

5. *Selected Messages*, 1: 121.

6. *Gospel Workers*, 507.

7. *Spalding-Magan Collection*, 231.

8. *Prophets and Kings*, 235.

# CHAPTER

# 13

# The Second Elijah—John the Baptist

John Wesley systematically toured Britain in the 1700s to preach God's Word in his spiritually famine-stricken country. In those days the state-appointed ministers were often more given to fox-hunting and card-playing than to soul-saving, thus leaving the people like sheep without a shepherd. Wesley came as a faithful undershepherd to seek and save the lost by pointing these neglected souls to Christ and ministering to them as Christ did.

He saturated the county of Cornwall with his message of hope to miners and herdsmen who had formerly dwelt in spiritual darkness and in the region of the shadow of death. Under the power of his ministry, whole villages were transformed—drunkenness, gambling, and vice ceased; church services and prayer meetings became well-attended. Decency, thrift, and good social order prevailed. Long after Wesley had passed from the scene, a visitor was touring the area. Struck by the tranquility and tidiness of the villages through which he passed, he stopped at several cottages to become acquainted with the people. Noticing in each one of these humble dwellings an identical portrait of a certain man, he asked an old miner at one of the cottages, "Whose picture is that?" Reverently taking off his hat, the miner replied, "There was a man sent from God, whose name was John."

He quoted a text that refers originally to John the Baptist. But his reply was apropos, because Wesley was a kind of latter-day John the Baptist. His labors not only brought great revival to the English-speaking world and beyond, but were also potently instrumental in keeping his country from plunging into anarchic rebellion against the old aristocratic order and inert religious system whose combined power almost completely suffocated the last breath of spiritual life in England.[1]

Life in eighteenth-century England and France was much alike. Poorly paid toil and social oppression were the lot of the common people. Rich landowners, constituting a small fraction of the population, conspicuously squandered the vast wealth they gained from the labors of the poor. France had its cynical philosophers Voltaire and Rousseau and the Marquis de Sade, whose life was devoted to bawdy exploits and shameless self-indulgence. Then came the Revolution and Reign of Terror.

But England had Wesley, Whitefield, and the Countess of Huntington, who devoted her ample resources to the furtherance of evangelistic preaching. The result was revival and the spread of foreign missions from the shores of Great Britain. Many secular historians attribute England's escape from a revolution, like that which gripped France, to the pervasive revival engendered by the Wesleys and their circuit-riding Methodist preachers. The influence of Methodism broke up the old order peacefully and paved the way for many social reforms such as improved prison conditions, the abolition of slave trafficking, fair labor laws, the institution of public education, and health care for the poor. All this happened despite the more than half-century of scorn and opposition the religious and social elite heaped on the Methodists for kindling so great a spiritual awakening.

Think of what God accomplished through the agency of one consecrated man, who had to labor against society's most formidable opponents, bishops, and nobility—the Pharisees and Sadducees of his day! Wesley achieved so much because he was filled with the Holy Spirit, filled with the life of Christ. He comprehended God's Word and taught it with clarity and a divine energy that went to the core of people's hearts.

His life resembled that of his earlier namesake, John the Baptist—the man who was sent from God (John 1:6). It is this calling and commission that makes all the difference in the life of every truly committed Christian. To know that one's life has a divinely appointed purpose drives us to seek God's presence and power and helps us keep steadily in view God's revealed will, so that we may live in cooperative partnership with Him.

As we study John the Baptist's life and work, let us remember that he was a type of what God's people are to be in the last days. "John the Baptist went forth in the spirit and power of Elijah to prepare the way of the Lord and to turn the people to the wisdom of the just. He was a representative of those living in these last days to whom God has entrusted sacred truths to present before the people to prepare the way for the second appearing of Christ."[2] Let us see how John's history parallels God's purpose for His final generation who are to bear witness to the Messiah's glory and imminent coming. This approach will bring the whole subject into sharply defined relevance to our life and times.

First, we remember the supremely significant closing prophecy of the Old Testament, "Behold, I will send you Elijah the prophet before the coming of the great and dreadful day of the Lord. And he will turn the hearts of the fathers to the children, and the hearts of the children to their fathers, lest I come and strike the earth with a curse" (Mal. 4:5, 6). These words were given to Israel to inspire them to prepare and look for a prophet who would usher in the time of the Messiah's appearing. This prophet is called "Elijah."

To every Hebrew mind in the years between Malachi (400s B.C.) and the Messiah's appearing, this would evoke powerful images of the intrepid reformer whose loyalty to God inspired him to overthrow Baal worship and lead the nation back to true worship. Careful students of Scripture would also seriously ponder the spiritual condition of Israel in their present days. They couldn't help but wonder if the promise of Elijah's reappearing would be associated with a new, perhaps deeper, more disguised form of idolatry among God's professed people. One thing was clear: When Elijah did come, the Messiah would not be far behind.

God did not leave the people in mystified suspense concerning the identity of the Messiah's prophesied forerunner. When the son of promise was due to come, the Lord sent Gabriel, His highest ranking angel, to announce his birth and restate his scripturally designated mission in richly amplified terms.

While the priest Zacharias was performing his temple duties at Jerusalem, an angel of the Lord appeared on the *right* side of the altar of incense, by his very position indicating the favor of God toward His people (Luke 1:11). Zacharias stood frightened and wonder-struck by the appearance of this celestial being.

"But the angel said to him, 'Do not be afraid, Zacharias, for your prayer is heard; and your wife Elizabeth will bear you a son, and you shall call his name John. And you will have joy and gladness, and many will rejoice at his birth. For he will be great in the sight of the Lord, and shall drink neither wine nor strong drink. He will also be filled with the Holy Spirit, even from his mother's womb. And he will turn many of the children of Israel to the Lord their God. He will also go before Him in the spirit and power of Elijah, "to turn the hearts of the fathers to the children," and the disobedient to the wisdom of the just, to make ready a people prepared for the Lord' " (Luke 1:13-17).

Gabriel did not say that John would be a literal reincarnation of Elijah but that he would conduct his mission "in the spirit and power of Elijah." His work would be *comparable* to that of Elijah, and he would perform it in the authority and strength of the Holy Spirit. To do this John must stay in close connection with God and be deeply instructed in His word.

John was to go forth as Jehovah's messenger, to bring men to the light of God. He must give a new direction to their thoughts. He must impress upon them the holiness of God's requirements, and their need of His perfect righteousness. Such a messenger must be holy. He must be a temple for the indwelling Spirit of God. In order to fulfill his mission he must have a sound physical constitution, and mental and spiritual strength. Therefore it would be necessary for him to control the appetites and passions. He must be able so to control his own powers that he could stand among men as unmoved by surrounding circumstances as the rocks and mountains of the wilderness.[3]

John was called to stand as a reformer in a time when materialism, sensual living, and moral degeneracy abounded. Further, the people's spiritual perceptions were benumbed by the coldheartedness and hollow ritualism of their religious leaders. Priests and worshipers idolized the types and ceremonies of Judaism, but Christ, the antitype to whom these religious services pointed, was not discerned or desired.

In some respects, therefore, John faced a subtler and more powerful challenge than did Elijah. John's spiritual predecessor had to contend with gross idolatry—Baal worship, with all its repulsive, demonic rituals, which stood in glaring contrast to the simple dignity of true Judaic worship. But John was called to dislodge people's hearts from a frozen orthodoxy, involving rigid adherence to Mosaic law blended with tedious rabbinic rules posing as advanced revelations of divine law. The ultimate effect of this perverted piety was to make the laws of God seem impossible to obey, and, consequently, impossible to respect.

Yet the people, sensing their sin and unworthiness, lived in gloomy terror of God and dread of their religious leaders. Thus their ideas of God were as false and warped as the more hedonistic and often carefree views of God held by the pagans. But the Lord would not allow such stifling spiritual bondage to continue forever.[4] Christ was coming to demolish the bulwarks of error, hypocrisy, and religious exploitation. He would replace the vast edifice of oppressive sanctimony with the cheering hope of His true gospel, made freely and lovingly available to all on an open field of mercy.

And John was raised up as His forerunner to prepare hearts for the blessing of so great salvation. What an honor! What a sacred task!

Gripped by the magnitude of his mission, John knew that he could not afford to squander his time or powers. Everything in his life must be directed to the accomplishment of his weighty calling that was so full of potential blessing for his nation and the world.

In the next chapter we will consider John's message and mission. We will also see how his character and chosen way of life fortified him to carry out his stupendously challenging assignment, under the direction of God.

*Questions for Discussion and Reflection*

1. Have you ever known a person who reminded you of John the Baptist? How? Describe the influence this person has had on your life.

2. After learning from Gabriel the spiritual mission their son John was to carry out, what effect do you suppose this had on the way his parents raised him?

3. How should parents who are faithful to God's Word raise their children today?

4. What changes would you like to see in yourself to make you a more inspiring and believable messenger of Christ's soon coming?

---

1. "When the ministry of John [the Baptist] began, the nation was in a state of excitement and discontent verging on revolution. . . . Amid discord and strife, a voice was heard from the wilderness, a voice startling and stern, yet full of hope: 'Repent ye; for the kingdom of heaven is at hand.' With a new, strange power it moved the people" (*The Desire of Ages*, 104). While the religious and civil authorities were too obtuse and self-inflated to recognize it, John's ministry actually helped to avert an insurrection by turning the people's thoughts to the need for spiritual regeneration as an even greater priority than improved social conditions. Had a revolt taken place, it would have been violently suppressed by the Romans, as it was in A.D. 70. Nothing would have been gained, and many lives would have been lost needlessly.

2. *Testimonies for the Church*, 3:61, 62.

3. *The Desire of Ages,* 100.

4. Perhaps the most moving and incisive description of the world's spiritual state just prior to the time of Christ's coming is found in *The Desire of Ages*, 34-38.

# CHAPTER
# 14

# John the Baptist's Training and Development

Deeply conscious of their son's calling, Zacharias and Elizabeth raised him in accordance with Gabriel's instructions. Like Samson, he was to drink neither wine nor strong drink. Unlike Samson, he held to this rule and rejoiced to be filled with the Holy Spirit instead of the benumbing pleasures of intemperance.

In his childhood and youth, John roamed in the wilderness, observing the mysteries of nature. Filled with the Holy Spirit from his mother's womb, John also no doubt saw in his desert haunts a reflection of the spiritual wilderness in which his nation dwelt. John's mind was nourished with Scripture, as his later preaching reveals. He searched the prophetic scrolls for a revelation of God and the plan of salvation. From its start John's whole life was a preparation for his future work. As with Christ's early years, the Bible is relatively silent about John's childhood, except to say that he "grew and became strong in spirit" (Luke 1:80).

What an ideal this presents for consecrated youth today! Adventist parents, knowing that they and their children are called to be God's witnesses, can fittingly believe that He wants their children to have a character preparation similar to that of John. A life as free as possible from artificial excitements and sensual indulgences will place any child on vantage ground for healthy development.

Luxurious, fashionable living is not the soil in which moral grandeur grows. To aid our children and youth in developing wholesomely, our church has established a system of schools worldwide dedicated to the principles and methods of true education. The object of our schools is spelled out in the book *Fundamentals of Christian Education*, by Ellen G. White.[1]

John's upbringing provides a valuable clue to the secret of his enormous influence in "turning the hearts of the fathers to the children and the hearts of the children to the fathers." When children are brought up unselfishly and trained to service, as John was, this helps create a strong and lasting bond in families.

Our age is rife with commercial interests that promote self-gratification, defiance of parental authority, indulgence of the lower nature, greed, and narcissistic identification with one's own age and peer group. All this divides and alienates family members from one another. Many a household (even among churchgoers) is plagued by a running battle between parents and children.

But what could bind families more closely together than a shared love for Jesus and a shared sense of mission in soul winning? It may seem old-fashioned, but it is certainly not foolish or out-of-date for parents to dedicate themselves and their children to serving God with pure devotion. Hannah so dedicated herself and her son Samuel, whose consecration to God left an immortal legacy of blessing to the world. From their infancy, Susanna Wesley dedicated John and all her other children to God's service and raised them in harmony with that resolve. Modern civilization has been incalculably blessed by the influence of this consecrated family. Men and women who have lived to the enduring benefit of humanity have all possessed a noble character. Character is not inherited. Conscious, informed choices that adhere to principle rise above adversities and turn liabilities into assets all go into character development.

A strong character is best developed from birth with the help of godly parents. But even those who lack this early advantage have access to the help of God, the Father of all. He is able to compensate for any deficiencies in our upbringing and fashion our characters in harmony with His own, if this is our desire.

By examining John the Baptist's character as portrayed in Scripture and the Spirit of Prophecy, we can gain insight into what sort of character God wants us to form for ourselves and foster in our children.

First, we should realize that John's special calling and commission did not exempt him from the struggles we all have in our earthborn natures. John also had natural imperfections of character and did not live a spiritually "charmed" life. He was not born with a golden halo over his head. Like Elijah, his ancient counterpart, John was a man subject to like passions as we are (James 5:17). "John had by nature the faults and weaknesses common to humanity; but the touch of divine love had transformed him."[2] This same touch of divine love is available to all of us for the asking.

"The work committed to [John the Baptist] was one demanding not only physical energy and endurance, but the highest qualities of mind and soul."[3] These qualities John cultivated by the same means that are available to all of us—prayer, Bible study, and careful observation of God's acts through nature and Providence.

In order to carry out his work in such a spiritual wilderness as Israel then was, John chose a simple, abstemious way of life, one that would keep his mind sharp and undistracted from his heaven-appointed work.[4] He chose to live in the desert away from the clamor of the world and close to nature, where he could contemplate God's way and works with little interference.[5]

John the Baptist in his desert life was taught of God. He studied the revelations of God in nature. Under the guiding of the Divine Spirit, he studied the scrolls of the prophets. By day and by night, Christ was his study, his meditation, until mind and heart and soul were filled with the glorious vision.

He looked upon the King in His beauty, and self was lost sight of. He beheld the majesty of holiness and knew himself to be inefficient and unworthy. It was God's message that he was to declare. It was in God's power and His righteousness that he was to stand. He was ready to go forth as Heaven's messenger, unawed by the human, because he had looked upon

97

the Divine. He could stand fearless in the presence of earthly monarchs, because with trembling he had bowed before the King of kings.[6]

John's name means "God is gracious." His mission was filled with gracious purpose, its central aim being to prepare the hearts of the people to receive the Prince of Peace, "full of grace and truth." Absorbed in communion with God, his own heart became richly imbued with Christ's spirit.

While recognizing that John did not casually mingle with society, it would be a mistake to view him as reclusive and antisocial. He guarded his powers and avoided trivial socializing, not because he despised humanity but to gather the strength he needed to make a soul-saving difference in people's lives. He did not wish his spiritual sensitivity to be blunted by needless contact with the sinful activities and conversation of the world and the controlling influence of false religious leaders. Surely there is a lesson in this for us. Few of us have adequate time alone with God. While we are not called on to live in isolation (and John bore no such message to the people), still we would do well to avoid absorption in radio and TV programs, video games, and shallow socializing that take up so much of people's time today. Our time alone with God should always include the purpose of gaining greater fitness to help others spiritually. This was John's constant goal.

> The life of John was not spent in idleness, in ascetic gloom, or in selfish isolation. From time to time he went forth to mingle with men; and he was ever an interested observer of what was passing in the world. From his quiet retreat he watched the unfolding of events. With vision illuminated by the divine Spirit he studied the characters of men, that he might understand how to reach their hearts with the message of heaven.[7]

Ponder this striking point. John carefully studied human nature so that he could find the most direct pathway to people's hearts, with the Holy Spirit's aid. He didn't approach his work as a dreamy mystic but with a disciplined mind and carefully considered plans. John's sensitivity to the world around him and powers of observation shine through the few fragments of his sermons recorded in Scripture (see Matt. 3:1-12; Luke 3:1-18; John 1:29-34; 3:27-36). They reveal how vividly he was in touch with the practical issues of life.

In John we find an instructive example to guide us in our efforts to reach the hearts of others with the gospel. We need to do more than learn sound doctrine. We must also study the most effective ways of reaching various human minds.

> In order to lead souls to Jesus there must be a knowledge of human nature and a study of the human mind. Much careful thought and fervent prayer are required to know how to approach men and women upon the great subject of truth.[8]

Could it be that a neglect of such careful study and prayerfulness of approach is one of the main reasons our witnessing efforts often bear so little fruit? Not that we should study popular psychology and secular methods of mind manipulation, but rather the scriptural view of the functions of the mind and God's methods of reaching the heart with sincerity and effectiveness. An excellent introduction to such study is the chapter "Mind Cure" in *The Ministry of Healing*, by Ellen G. White. This chapter presents a wealth of Scripture to help soul winners reach troubled minds that need the healing influences of God's Word. A more extensive study of human psychology from heaven's perspective is given in the superb two-volume E. G. White compilation, *Mind, Character, and Personality*.

If we followed John the Baptist's method of studying the human mind, we would not use clumsy, heavy-handed approaches to communicate the message of truth, nor would we use adroitly sensational tactics just because they might give an appearance of quick success. Our work for the Lord must bear the impress of "Christ's method alone." By studying His methods, we will become sensitized to the most tactful, considerate, and perceptive ways of ministering to human needs and explaining truth.

So filled was John with the Spirit of Jesus, that all Judea suspensefully mused as to whether he might be the promised Messiah (Luke 3:15). His very words were often a near-counterpart to those that Christ spoke during His ministry.[9]

In our next chapter we will look at more of the particulars of John's inaugural ministry that electrified all Judea with keen anticipation of the Messiah's appearing.

*Questions for Discussion and Reflection*

1. What lessons does John's childhood and early life have for parents and children today?

2. What can we learn from John's chosen lifestyle about how to be "in the world but not of the world," i.e., useful to the world without being contaminated by worldly customs and culture? Include in your consideration John's temperate lifestyle and abstemious diet.

3. Why is it important to understand the human mind in order to lead people to Christ?

4. What are the dangers of popular psychology, including hypnotism, subliminal perception, mind control, and humanistic methods of psychoanalysis?

---

1. Other valuable studies in this line by the same author are *Education, Counsels to Parents, Teachers, and Students*, and large portions of *Testimonies for the Church*, volume 6. They are highly recommended to the reader. Ellen White's philosophy of education is epitomized in the following two statements:

"In the highest sense the work of education and the work of redemption are one, for in education, as in redemption, 'other foundation can no man lay than that is laid, which is Jesus Christ'" (*Education*, 30).

"True education does not ignore the value of scientific knowledge or literary acquirements; but above information it values power; above power, goodness; above intellectual requirements, character" (Ibid., 225).

2. *Gospel Workers*, 55.

3. *The Ministry of Healing*, 379.

4. Temperance in eating and drinking has a far greater influence on character development than many are willing to admit. Consider 1 Corinthians 10:31; and Proverbs 23:2. "You need clear, energetic minds, in order to appreciate the exalted character of the truth, to value the atonement, and to place a right estimate upon eternal things. If you pursue a wrong course, and indulge wrong habits of eating, and thereby weaken the intellectual powers, you will not place that high estimate upon salvation and eternal life which will inspire you to conform your life to the life of Christ; you will not make those earnest, self-sacrificing efforts for entire conformity to the will of God, which His word requires, and which are necessary to give you a moral fitness for the finishing touch of immortality" (*Testimonies for the Church*, 2:66). Also see *The Sanctified Life*, 18-33.

5. See Mark 1:4; Luke 1:80; *The Desire of Ages*, 101; *Testimonies for the Church*, 4:108, 109. Consider this penetrating observation by a young English minister who lived from 1830–1861. "The men who have left the impress of their own individuality most markedly on the world—men of striking independence of character—have mostly been trained in solitude:—take such instances as the histories of Moses, Elijah, and John. In the rushing life of cities, men are moulded by the spirit of the time: in the loneliness of nature, they learn to feel more deeply the power of conscience and of God—to live in the eternal, not in the transient" (E. L. Hull, *Sermons Preached at King's Lynn*, First Series, 9th ed. [London: Nisbet, 1873], 138).

6. *Testimonies for the Church*, 8:331, 332.

7. *The Desire of Ages*, 102.

8. *Testimonies for the Church*, 4:67.

9. For example, compare John 3:29-33 with Matthew 25:1; John 3:11, 13, 18; 6:26-29, 40, 47; 5:20; 8:23, 26; 15:15.

# CHAPTER
# 15

# John the Baptist's Message and Mission

Excepting Christ, the Prince of prophets, never in the history of God's people had any prophet's work been so clearly foretold and defined as was that of John. His commission is blazed forth in words of fire that flash with poetry and drama, while they ring also with solid purpose. Closing the record of the Old Testament and opening the door into the New, Malachi predicted the appearance of the Messiah's forerunner. "'Behold, I will send you Elijah the prophet before the coming of the great and dreadful day of the Lord. And he will turn the hearts of the fathers to the children, and the hearts of the children to their fathers, lest I come and strike the earth with a curse'" (Mal. 4:5, 6). Gabriel referred to this prophecy in announcing the birth of John to his father, Zacharias: "'He will also go before Him [God] in the spirit and power of Elijah, "to turn the hearts of the fathers to the children" and the disobedient to the wisdom of the just, to make ready a people prepared for the Lord'" (Luke 1:17). From Malachi's prophecy and Gabriel's interpretation of it, we find that as the Messiah's forerunner, John had a threefold calling. His was a work of *restoration, reconciliation,* and *preparation.* Each of these three distinct but closely related features of his mission to advance the kingdom of heaven deserves particular study.

*Restoration.* John's work was to restore truth in its unalloyed purity. In John's day, rabbinic wisdom was exalted above Scripture, and pagan ideas had infiltrated Judaism. The resulting mixture produced a grossly distorted view of God that portrayed Him as stern, exacting, merciless, and materialistic. Ritualism had taken the place of relationship with God, and human traditions had supplanted divine law. John's work was to clear away this rubble of sanctimonious error and thus liberate the people to recognize Jesus as the Messiah. He laid the ax to the root of deception's tree, so that truth could spring up in all its native vigor and fruitfulness.

Until John's appearance, everything in Judaism as it then stood was designed to turn people's thoughts away from the character and work of Israel's Redeemer. The religion they practiced in God's name was a virtual denial of His attributes and purposes; thus it was a colossal sham and a formidable obstruction to becoming truly acquainted with God. He was seen as someone to be dreaded and appeased rather than trusted and loved. John called people not to rituals but repentance, not to traditions but truth that could be obeyed through divine grace.

His hearers, while not flattered by his words, were stirred with new hope. John did not present God as indulgent and permissive, but he did reveal that God is approachable and forgiving, that He is a restorer of degraded, broken lives. This was something new in Israel. Such a voice of hope had not been heard since the days of prophets like Isaiah, Ezekiel, and Zechariah. Those who truly thirsted for redemption recognized the divine authority of the man clad in camel skins, whose simple life contrasted starkly with the affluence and haughty sophistication of the temple rulers. No wonder Jesus said, "'John came to you in the way of righteousness, and you did not believe him; but tax collectors and harlots believed him'" (Matt. 21:32). John reached the hearts of society's outcasts and its least respected members, such as Roman soldiers, tax collectors, and common laborers. The very people who would seem to have been the most hardened to spiritual concerns melted under the power of his preaching; their hearts were kindled with a new hope and a new vision of God. John spoke of God in a way that led people to open their hearts to the full light of the gospel. "There was a man sent from

God, whose name was John. This man came for a witness, to bear witness of the Light, that all through him might believe" (John 1:6, 7). This mission was as central to the work of restoration as any calling could be, and according to Jesus, John carried out this work with entire faithfulness (see Matt. 17:11-13).

> With no elaborate arguments or finespun theories did John declare his message. Startling and stern, yet full of hope, his voice was heard from the wilderness: "Repent ye: for the kingdom of heaven is at hand." Matthew 3:2. With a new, strange power it moved the people. The whole nation was stirred. Multitudes flocked to the wilderness.[1]

John and his disciples offered baptism to every repentant believer. This act signified entrance into God's kingdom, and everyone who was willing to accept God's simple terms and renewing grace was eligible for the benefit. By teaching the way of holiness as defined in Scripture, John became a restorer of paths to dwell in. He faithfully fulfilled his prophesied commission to "'give light to those who sit in darkness and the shadow of death, to guide our feet into the way of peace'" (Luke 1:79).

*Reconciliation.* Sin alienates people from God. Perverted religion helps people further barricade their hearts against the Lord, while projecting a semblance of devotion and piety. It was this double wall of resistance that John was enabled to penetrate. He did this not by assaulting the religious leaders but by turning people's attention to the Lamb of God, who alone can take away the sin of the world.

> In simplicity and plainness, he pointed out the errors and crimes of men. . . . He flattered none; neither would he receive flattery of any. . . . His discernment of character and spiritual sight read the purposes and hearts of those who came to him, and he fearlessly told, both rich and poor, the honorable and the lowly, that without repentance of their sins, and a thorough conversion, although they might claim to be righteous, they could not enjoy the favor of God, and

have part in the Kingdom of the Messiah, whose coming he announced.[2]

"'And *he will turn* many of the children of Israel to the Lord their God'" (Luke 1:16). It was this grand work of reconciliation that made John such a towering figure and gave such compelling force to his ministry.

Some writers have suggested that John overstepped his mission when he reproved Herod and that he could have been spared martyrdom if he had been less confrontational with those in authority. This betrays a misconception of the man and his mission. Far from being an abrasive meddler, John spoke under the inspiration and prompting of God. He operated in the spirit and power of Elijah, and it would be folly to charge him with speaking too pointedly.

*Early Writings* gives us valuable insight into the circumstances in which John delivered his testimony of warning to Herod:

> Herod was affected as he listened to the powerful, pointed testimonies of John, and with deep interest he inquired what he must do to become his disciple. John was acquainted with the fact that he was about to marry his brother's wife, while her husband was yet living, and faithfully told Herod that this was not lawful. Herod was unwilling to make any sacrifice. He married his brother's wife, and through her influence, seized John and put him in prison, intending however to release him.[3]

How Herod's intention became derailed is well known. Intemperance, infatuation, and fear of lost favor among his dissolute courtiers made him yield to Herodias and Salome's vile request to have John's head on a platter. This cruel treatment no more invalidates John's faithfulness in reproving sin than Jesus' crucifixion calls into question the advisability of His rebukes to the priests and scribes. If we are not clear on this point, we shall be constantly tempted to muffle our witness and shun our duty to faithfully warn the erring and denounce sin.

"In this fearful time, just before Christ is to come the second time, God's faithful preachers will have to bear a still more pointed testimony than was borne by John the Baptist."[4]

> They are not to speak their own words, but words which One greater than the potentates of earth has bidden them speak. Their message is to be "Thus saith the Lord." God calls for men like Elijah, Nathan, and John the Baptist— men who will bear His message with faithfulness, regardless of the consequences; men who will speak the truth bravely, though it call for the sacrifice of all they have.[5]

Plain speaking, done in the love of God and with a genuine burden for the salvation of souls, does not offend the honest of heart. They sense the genuineness of the concerns expressed and are far more likely to repent of sin and turn to God than if they hear smooth, flattering words. "Open rebuke is better than love carefully concealed. Faithful are the wounds of a friend, but the kisses of an enemy are deceitful" (Prov. 27:5, 6). How many souls have gone down to eternal ruin, unreconciled to God, who might have been saved if they had been faithfully warned and reproved by those who saw their sins but were too timid or cautious to speak a timely word of warning. Such friends have neglected the duty specified in Isaiah 58:1, 2.

> The true people of God, who have the spirit of the work of the Lord and the salvation of souls at heart, will ever view sin in its real, sinful character. They will always be on the side of faithful and plain dealing with the sins which easily beset the people of God. Especially in the closing work for the church, in the sealing time of the one hundred and forty-four thousand who are to stand without fault before the throne of God, will they feel most deeply the wrongs of God's professed people.[6]

Consider this quotation in the light of Ezekiel 9, and its significance will become more apparent.

Warning and reproof are the most delicate part of a ministry of reconciliation. Those having "the spirit of the work of the Lord and the salvation of souls at heart," as did John the Baptist and Elijah, are the best able to effectively remonstrate with the erring. Indignant at hypocrisy, John graciously received all who turned to the Lord with sincerity of heart. He plainly showed the people that reconciliation to God called for the inworking of divine grace to purify the life. His influence to carry out this work was prophesied at his birth; see Luke 1:68-75.

> He saw his people deceived, self-satisfied, and asleep in their sins. He longed to rouse them to a holier life. The message that God had given him to bear was designed to startle them from their lethargy, and cause them to tremble because of their great wickedness. Before the seed of the gospel could find lodgment, the soil of the heart must be broken up. Before they would seek healing from Jesus, they must be awakened to their danger from the wounds of sin.[7]

Responding to the Spirit's powerful witness through him, multitudes flocked to the wilderness to hear John. "Many were brought to repentance, and received baptism. Persons of all ranks submitted to the requirement of the Baptist, in order to participate in the kingdom he announced."[8]

As an ambassador for Christ, John pled with people to be reconciled to God on God's own terms, and the Lord granted him enormous success in carrying out this commission. Turning the disobedient to the wisdom of the just, John carried out a ministry of reconciliation on the highest level.

*Preparation.* In defining John's prophetic mission to Zacharias, Gabriel declared that Christ's forerunner was called "to make ready a people prepared for the Lord" (Luke 1:17). John's keen awareness of this charge found expression in his first public utterances. Matthew and Luke describe the force of his ministry in the words of Isaiah, "The voice of one crying in the wilderness: 'Prepare the way of the Lord, make His paths straight. Every valley shall be filled and every mountain and hill brought low; the crooked places shall be made straight and the rough ways smooth; and all flesh shall see the salvation of God' " (Luke 3:4-6; cf. Matt. 3:1-3).

John's whole life was consumed with one objective—preparing the way for people to receive the Messiah as Savior and Lord so that they could be fit subjects for His kingdom. At this time the Jews were very "kingdom" conscious. They hated Rome, to which they were in subjugation, and looked forward to the Messiah's appearing to expel the Roman power and exalt Israel. Their thinking on this subject was deeply flawed.

John and Jesus pointed out that fitness for the Messiah's kingdom involved a complete transformation of character, which could be brought about only through repentance and the regenerative work of the Holy Spirit. Israel's call was not to political greatness but to individual and collective godliness that drew its power from constant submission to the Redeemer's lordship. It was a kingdom of love and righteousness that demanded—and offered—renovation of soul for all its subjects.

Self-righteous people who wanted to hate others and exalt themselves found John's message offensive, vexing, and impertinent. They could not completely ignore the Holy Spirit's power, which surcharged John's preaching and gave such majestic force to his character. But they were angry over his denunciation of the sins and pride that were so vital a part of their religious ideas and practices. The idea that they needed to repent and make preparation for the Messiah's appearing seemed like an insult, an impudent outrage. How dare this untutored, outlandish man, this wilderness hermit, tell them, the erudite guardians of the law, what to do!

"Who are you? What do you say of yourself?" they asked, hardly able to conceal their annoyance and fear. "Are you Christ or Elijah?" With ringing forthrightness, John answered, "I am the voice of one crying in the wilderness, make straight the way of the Lord, as said the prophet Isaiah."

"Well, then, if you are not Christ or Elijah, why are you baptizing people?" (That is, "Presumptuous man, who gave you authority to do this thing? What do you mean by calling people to repentance and usurping our authority by your preaching?")

Clothed in divine authority, John answered without wavering, "I baptize with water, but there stands among you One whom you do not recognize. He it is whose coming is preferred before me, whose shoe's latchet I am not worthy to unloose." This answer left his inquisitors stunned and speechless.

The next day as John saw Jesus approaching, he had the privilege of pointing out the One of whom he spoke, "Behold the Lamb of God," he declared, "which takes away the sin of the world." John's reply revealed the taproot of his spiritual power. He offered no vindication of himself but pointed to the Lamb of God. This is the missing element in all loveless, legalistic reformations. To magnify the Lamb of God, not just in word but in the power of a life that reflects His virtue, is our work till the close of time.[9]

A steadfast beholding of the Lamb, combined with faithful obedience to His word is the best preparation we can obtain for membership in His kingdom. John promised that Christ would baptize His people with the Holy Spirit and with fire. This fiery baptism consumes the dross in our characters and imparts to us the very life of Christ. His word, His Spirit, and His blood combine to make us strong in the power of His might. Thus we have all our springs in Him, and in our hearts are the highways to Zion (Ps. 87:7; 84:5, ASV). We mature as a people prepared for the coming of the Lord.

But just as in John's day some resented the idea of needing to prepare for the Messiah's coming, in our time many professed believers reject the idea of needing to gain any further preparation once they declare faith in Christ as their Savior. To them the idea of "preparation" smacks of righteousness by works. But such need to consider the great kingdom parables of Jesus—the man without a wedding garment; the ten virgins; the talents. In these parables Jesus was not teaching legalism but conscientious commitment to Him and His cause. Salvation involves more than pardon and release from sin; it also includes discipleship and devotion to the furtherance of God's kingdom.[10] Jesus warned nominal believers who know God's will and do not prepare themselves for His coming to expect punishment rather than reward in the day of final reckoning (see Luke 12:47, 48).

When Jesus comes back the second time, it will be to gather to Himself a people who have prepared for that event by availing themselves of every offered blessing of the gospel, which strengthened them to actively participate in advancing His kingdom, just as John did. Their preparation is a work of cooperative response to divine grace, untainted with self-merit (see Phil. 2:12, 13). "Let us be glad and rejoice, and give honor to him: for the marriage of the Lamb is come, and His wife hath *made herself ready*. And to her was granted that she should be arrayed in fine linen, clean and white: for the fine linen is the righteousness of saints" (Rev. 19:7, 8, KJV; emphasis supplied). These saints are not skillful weavers of their own righteousness (that would be a blasphemous imposture) but grateful recipients of Christ and His righteousness,[11] which purifies their hearts and remains uncontaminated by the human agent upon whom it is bestowed, for "His righteousness endures forever" (Ps. 112:9). It is everlasting and brings in everlasting life.

*Questions for Discussion and Reflection*

1. In what ways was John the Baptist a "burning and shining light"? Why did many people rejoice in his light? John 5:35 (cf. Dan. 12:3, 4; John 1:8, 9).

2. Read John 10:41, 42 and answer the following two questions. What results from John the Baptist's ministry were even greater than the working of miracles? Where did John receive the wisdom that made it possible for him to speak only what was true about Christ?

3. What was the role of the Holy Spirit in John's life and ministry? See Luke 1:13-17; John 3:27-34.

4. Using an unabridged Bible concordance, discover how God's people are to prepare for Christ's coming kingdom of glory. (Look up the words *prepare, preparation, ready.*)

---

1. *Testimonies for the Church*, 8:332.

2. *Review and Herald*, 7 January 1873.

3. *Early Writings*, 154.

4. *Testimonies for the Church*, 1:321.

5. *Prophets and Kings*, 142.

6. *Testimonies for the Church*, 3:266.

7. *The Desire of Ages*, 103, 104.

8. Ibid., 105.

9. Charles Spurgeon, a champion soul winner, observed, "The best training for a soul-saving minister is precisely that which he would follow if his sole object were to develop the character of Christ in himself. The better the man, the more powerful will his preaching become. As he grows like Jesus, he will preach like Jesus. Given like purity of motive, tenderness of heart, and clearness of faith, and you will have like force of utterance. The direct road to success in saving souls is to become like the Saviour. The imitation of Christ is the true art of sacred rhetoric" (C. H. Spurgeon, *My Sermon Notes* [London: Marshall Brothers, Ltd., 1886], 14).

10. "The forgiveness of sins is not the sole result of the death of Jesus. He made the infinite sacrifice, not only that sin might be removed, but that human nature might be restored, rebeautified, reconstructed from its ruins, and made fit for the presence of God" *(Testimonies for the Church*, 5:537). Read the whole chapter "Practical Godliness," 532-541.

11. "This robe, woven in the loom of heaven, has in it not one thread of human devising. Christ in His humanity wrought out a perfect character, and this character He offers to impart to us" (*Christ's Object Lessons*, 311).

# CHAPTER
# 16

# John's Enduring Legacy

About the year 1785, in a large seaport on England's west coast, a notice was sent out inviting the townspeople to assemble and hear a preacher who was becoming famous for the power and depth of his messages. Many gathered to hear him in the city's largest church. The preacher read his text and was about to begin his sermon when he stopped and leaned his head on the pulpit, remaining silent for a few moments. The audience worried, thinking he might have gotten sick and was unable to go on. But then he lifted his head and looked full at the congregation, seeming to study every face. He said, "Before I begin my message, I would like to tell you a personal experience. It's now exactly fifteen years ago since I last stood within this place of worship. Then, as now, you had a visiting preacher, which many of you came to hear. The church was full. Among the company were three rough fellows, each about twenty years old. Armed with rocks hidden in their pockets, they came to disturb the meeting. They planned to fling the rocks at the preacher when he came to some particularly stirring part of his sermon, so that they could destroy the whole effect by frightening him off the stage. After a while one of the three ruffians said, 'I've had enough of this old bore—throw!' Another of the fellows restrained him and said, 'No, let's hear him come to his point first.'

After a few minutes he drew out a rock and hissed, 'Enough, let's get started.' The third troublemaker interposed, saying, 'It would be better to give up this idea. I'm not going to throw any rocks today and neither should you.' Shooting looks of disgust at him, his two companions left, muttering curses. The third man stayed to hear the rest of the message."

The preacher drew a deep breath and continued, "Now, my brethren, I wish to tell you of the different fates of these three men. Not long afterwards, the first was hanged at Tyburn, for his crimes. The second is imprisoned in this city, awaiting execution for murder. And the third,"—here the preacher paused, wiping sweat from his brow—"now stands before you to preach the gospel that has restored his soul. Listen to him!"

That preacher's ministry among them for the next few days brought about a great revival in the entire city.

Restoration is the very essence of the gospel. It restores the dignity, worth, and wholeness of life that Satan has taken away. It restores fractured relationships. It restores health and peace. It restores our souls. It also restores all truth which, for earth's 6,000-year history, Satan has targeted for distortion and destruction. Satan fears nothing so much as for God's Word to become fully known to us and take soul-saving effect in our lives. Jesus prayed on our behalf to His Father, "Sanctify them by Your truth, Your word is truth" (John 17:17). From this Satan can easily deduce that just as truth sanctifies, error debases the human soul. Therefore he has crowded a multitude of errors into the creeds of Christendom.

But it is God's purpose to restore all truth, so that we might have an unadulterated revelation of His Word that saves and purifies our souls. Satan specializes in taking away those truths that seem the least important, the least necessary to restore. But in God's revelation, nothing is insignificant. In well-designed machinery, every nut and bolt counts. About fifteen years ago a passenger plane crashed because a bolt that fastened the engine to its housing came loose. None of the surviving families of the hundred or more people killed in that crash would have called that loosened bolt unimportant.

John's mission was to restore truth, truth that had its source and destination in Christ, who is the way, the truth, and the life. Since the days of John people have been pressing ardently into the kingdom of heaven, determined to let no traditions, fallacies, or sins in their own hearts prevail against the grace and truth of Jesus. John's spiritual legacy to God's remnant people is profound and enduring. Let's quickly survey its leading features.

*Loyalty to God's Word.* Carnal religion has long engaged in deadly combat between two equally unprofitable positions, which are both in opposite ways legalistic. The first position is cold, sterile orthodoxy that regards salvation as the reward of determined compliance with God's law. This is conservative legalism. The second makes a lucky charm of faith, which is seen as the magical passkey to heaven, irrespective of the believer's character or conduct. By reducing faith to a forensic technicality (instead of seeing it for what it is—a divinely enabling power), the result is liberal legalism.

Ancient Israel was plagued with both kinds of legalism, and so is modern Christendom.[1] John did not occupy a midway position between liberal and conservative legalism. His position was categorically different and far higher. He taught no false dichotomy between faith and works but advocated a *faith that works by love and cleanses the soul.* For him faith in God was a divine gift, an agency through which the power of the truth may be appropriated and enacted in the life through the impartation of the Spirit. This position corresponds to that of all the Bible prophets, who firmly believed in power of God's grace to give us happy, warm, intimate communion with Him, combined with divinely granted power to obey His law and requirements. (See, for example, Deut 30:10-14; Isa. 26:12; 57:14, 15; Jer 31:33, 34; Ezek. 36:25-29; Mic. 7:8, 9, 18-20; Zech. 3:1-8.) The list of texts could be lengthened, but this sampling may suffice. It's not "Love *or* obedience, which will it be?" but the joyful obedience of supernatural love, an obedience that deepens as love matures (Ps. 119:32-41, 102-104, 171-176). The apostle John summarized this concept well in one verse: "Whoso keepeth His word, in him verily is the love of God perfected: hereby we know that we are in Him" (1 John 2:5).

John the Baptist reflected in his experience and teachings healthy

Bible religion (John 3:27-34). "What was it that made John the Baptist great? He closed his mind to the mass of tradition presented by the teachers of the Jewish nation, and opened it to the wisdom which comes from above."[2] Honoring the supremacy of Christ, John rejected unscriptural traditions no matter how sanctimonious or deeply entrenched they were and ascribed all authority to God's word. He testified that his joy was fulfilled to hear the Bridegroom's voice—the voice that he had faithfully followed during all his brief but intensely devoted life.

*Temperance and simplicity of life.* John ate an abstemious diet, drank no wine, dressed simply, and chose to dwell in natural surroundings. "He was a representative of those living in the last days, to whom God has entrusted sacred truths to present before the people, to prepare the way for the second appearing of Christ. And the same principles of temperance which John practiced should be observed by those who in our day are to warn the world of the coming of the Son of man."[3]

It is ironic that John, an exemplar of temperance, was the victim of a death inspired by intemperance. This allegorically typifies the reason for which God's final remnant will be persecuted. Those who are spiritually drunk from the wine of Babylon's wrathful fornication will be incensed toward those who "speak forth the words of truth and soberness," in the powerful warning of the three angels' messages (see Acts 26:25 and Rev. 14:6-12).

*Refusal to be drawn into controversy.* It was inevitable that controversy should swirl around so pure and powerful a reformer as John. When challenged by the religious leaders, he would not argue about his identity but simply declared himself to be the person he was—Christ's forerunner, not to be the center of attention but simply the one who helped prepare people to recognize and receive the Lamb of God, who came to save the world.

John would not become embroiled in controversy about baptism in contrast to rabbinic modes of ceremonial purification but once again pointed people to Christ, the purifier of hearts, the giver of every perfect gift. John was secure in his identity; he knew that he had a great and important work to do, but he did not consider himself a great and important man. Thus it has always been with

God's faithful servants. They do not underestimate the sacredness of their calling, but they also do not regard themselves as exceptional people worthy of admiration. Their whole desire is to attract people to Christ and serve Him in whatever ways His providence directs.

This truth is exemplified in an exchange between two men. "Brother [Alfred S.] Hutchins was at one time riding in Vermont and he met a lawyer. 'Well,' said the lawyer, 'I understand that you are a Seventh-day Adventist.' 'Yes.' 'Well,' said he, 'you are nothing but little men.' 'Yes, we know that,' said Brother Hutchins, 'but we are handling mighty subjects. It is by the study of these mighty subjects that we are trying to get the truth before the people.' "[4]

*Self-effacement.* After Leonardo Da Vinci had completed his painting, "The Last Supper," a friend visited him to see the work. "That goblet is wonderful"; remarked the friend, "it stands out like solid silver!" Shocked by this observation, Da Vinci immediately dashed his brush over the goblet and exclaimed, "Nothing shall draw the eye of the beholder from my Lord!" This illustrates John's character. His whole desire was to exalt Christ. "He who comes after me is preferred before me, for He was before me." "One mightier than I is coming, whose sandal strap I am not worthy to loose"; and "He must increase, but I must decrease" (John 1:15; Luke 3:16; John 3:30). John gladly saw his own ministry superseded, or, rather, fulfilled as his disciples and converts followed Christ. John had no jealousy and well realized that his work was not sufficient to lay the foundation of the Christian church. His "unselfish joy in the ministry of Christ presents the highest type of nobility ever revealed in man."[5]

John's humility typifies the humility of those who bear the final message of warning to the world.

Truly great men are invariably modest. Humility is a grace which sits naturally upon them as a garment. Those who have stored their minds with useful knowledge, and who possess genuine attainments and refinement, are the ones who will be most willing to admit the weakness of their own understanding. They are not self-confident nor boastful; but in view of the higher attainments to which they might rise in intellectual greatness, they seem to themselves to have but just begun the ascent. It is the superficial thinker, the one who has but a beginning or smattering of knowledge, who deems himself wise and takes on disgusting airs of importance.[6]

As we have clearer views of truth, we have humbler views of self. Thomas Aquinas (1227–1274) shortly before his death entered into a deep state of joyous contemplation. When he emerged from it, he refused to sit as his desk and finish his masterwork *Summa Theologica*. This puzzled his friends, who thought that he should strive to bring such a "great" work to completion. Aquinas's secretary asked, "My father, why have you cast aside so great a work which you began for the glory of God and the illumination of the world?" His reply was brief and decisive, "It's not possible. I cannot write any more." When pressed to explain why, Aquinas simply said, "Everything that I have written appears to me as simply rubbish." At the time he broke off writing, he had been treating the theme of the nature and work of Christ as well as the church's sacraments. Aquinas's evaluation of his work was correct, because he had a very weak grasp of Christ as a personal Savior and saw Him more as a revealer of new knowledge than as the Creator of a new heart. Perhaps in his last days Aquinas came to know Christ savingly.

All who meet Christ as a personal Savior will recognize that the most and best they have done or could do is very little in comparison to the infinite greatness of what Christ has done. This realization excludes boasting and pride. All our work, henceforth, is a humble thank offering to Him rather than a self-glorifying venture.

*Call to repentance, holiness and prayer.* John's religion was the embodiment of practicality. For him real godliness translated into morally upright living. Any religion that offers less than this is worse than worthless; it is a disillusioning sham that will turn skeptical observers into sneering cynics. When asked by the common people what they should do, John said, "If you have two coats, give the extra one to someone who has none." To the tax collectors he said,

"Demand no more tax than what is legally due." To the soldiers he said, "Do violence to none, accuse no one falsely, and be satisfied with your pay." John did not equate ethical living with salvation, but he affirmed that true salvation results in honest, upright living and repentance of all evil conduct. The world has the right to expect this, and Christians should demand this of themselves.

> The work of reformation here brought to view by John, the purging of heart and mind and soul, is one that is needed by many who today profess to have the faith of Christ. Wrong practices that have been indulged in need to be put away; the crooked paths need to be made straight, and the rough places smooth. The mountains and hills of self-esteem and pride need to be brought low. There is need of bringing forth "fruits meet for repentance." When this work is done in the experience of God's believing people, "all flesh shall see the salvation of God."[7]

John also was a man of deep prayer, who taught his disciples to pray (Luke 11:1).

*Emphasis on the Lamb.* John clearly saw that purity of life sprang not from moral resolve but from the power of the Atonement (John 1:29, 26). His exaltation of Christ as the Lamb of God imbued his ministry with supreme grace and power.

> Looking in faith to the Redeemer, John had risen to the height of self-abnegation. He sought not to attract men to himself, but to lift their thoughts higher and still higher, until they should rest upon the Lamb of God. . . .
>
> Those who are true to their calling as messengers for God will not seek honor for themselves. Love for self will be swallowed up in love for Christ. They will recognize that it is their work to proclaim, as did John the Baptist, "Behold the lamb of God, which taketh away the sin of the world."[8]

The glorious influence of this emphasis was strikingly demonstrated by an experience in Charles H. Spurgeon's work. Invited to preach in 1857 at London's Crystal Palace, Spurgeon visited the auditorium to test its acoustic properties and select a good location for the speaker's platform. Standing in the place that seemed best, Spurgeon richly intoned, "Behold the Lamb of God, which taketh away the sin of the world." In one of the galleries a workman, who knew nothing of the speaker's presence, heard these mighty words. They pierced his soul as a message sent from heaven. Smitten with conviction, he put down his tools and went home to pray. After hours of intense struggle, he found peace and salvation in contemplating Christ in His innocence and purity, dying as a sacrifice to save guilty sinners. After hearing him speak publicly, the workman told Spurgeon how this one verse that broke upon him in so startling a way had become the means of his salvation.

*Emphasis on the Holy Spirit's work.* Not many of John the Baptist's words are recorded in Scripture, but a notable proportion of them deal with the Holy Spirit. John saw the Spirit as the great ignitor, purifier, and invigorator of spiritual life (Luke 3:16; John 3:34). Moreover he saw the Spirit as the supreme Witness who authenticated and magnified Jesus as the Messiah (John 1:32-34). John's emphasis on the Spirit corresponds to what ours should be.

> As never before we must pray for the Holy Spirit to be more abundantly bestowed upon us, and we must look for its sanctifying influence to come upon the workers, that those for whom they labor may know that they have been with Jesus and have learned of Him.
>
> We need spiritual eyesight, that we may see the designs of the enemy, and as faithful watchmen proclaim the danger. We need power from above, that we may understand, as far as the human mind can, the great themes of Christianity and their far-reaching principles.
>
> Those who are under the influence of the Spirit of God, will not be fanatical, but calm and steadfast, free from extravagance in thought, word, or deed. Amid the confusion of delusive doctrines, the Spirit of God will be a guide and a shield to those who have not resisted the evidences of truth, silencing every other voice but that which comes from Him who is the truth.[9]

It is the Spirit that causes to shine into darkened minds the bright beams of the Sun of Righteousness; that makes men's hearts burn within them with an awakened realization of the truths of eternity; that presents before the mind the great standard of righteousness, and convinces of sin; that inspires faith in Him who alone can save from sin; that works to transform character by withdrawing the affections of men from those things which are temporal and perishable, and fixing them upon the eternal inheritance. The Spirit recreates, refines, and sanctifies human beings, fitting them to become members of the royal family, children of the heavenly King. [10]

As the end of time draws near, our need for the Holy Spirit increases, both to fortify us for preaching the gospel with heavenly anointing and to protect us from the advanced delusions and proliferating heresies of these last days. The restless spirit of humanity is always trying to come up with something innovative, especially for the purpose of getting fame and securing followers. This involves downplaying or denying some established truths and magnifying private opinions as great revelations which previous Christian leaders never saw. How important that must make the discoverer of these new and brilliant ideas! Paul warned the Ephesian elders of this destructive development (see Acts 20:28-32).

The church at Ephesus and the whole Christian church toward the close of the apostolic era was severely harmed by just such proceedings. Christ's message to Sardis closely resembled the tenor of His message to Ephesus. Both churches had lost their first love, both were dying spiritually. But Sardis sought to remedy the problem by generating new ideas that would bring creative force and fresh impetus to the gospel message. What was the problem? Had the gospel gotten old? Was it beginning to creak and totter toward obsolescence? Far from it. Christians themselves had become complacent, apathetic, and lazy. The gospel imparted no life to them because they were disconnecting from Christ, the Author of the gospel (see 2 Cor. 4:3, 4).

One after another of the old standard-bearers had fallen, and some had become wearied of the oft-repeated truths. They desired a new phase of doctrine, more pleasing to many minds. They thought they needed a wonderful change, and in their spiritual blindness did not discern that their sophistries would uproot all the experiences of the past. . . .

But the Lord could see the end from the beginning. Through John [the Revelator] He sent them the warning, "Remember therefore how thou hast received and heard, and hold fast, and repent. If therefore thou shalt not watch, I will come on thee as a thief."

Among the people to whom this message was sent, there were those who had heard and been convinced by the preaching of John the Baptist, but who had lost the faith in which they once rejoiced. There were others who had received the truth from Christ's teaching, and who were once ardent believers, but who had lost their first love, and were without spiritual strength. They had not held the beginning of their confidence firm unto the end. They had a name to live, but as far as exerting a saving influence is concerned, they were dead. They had a form of godliness without the power. They quibbled about matters of no special importance, not given by the Lord as tests, till these matters became as mountains, separating them from Christ and from one another. [11]

John the Baptist's ministry as a restorer reminds us that we have no need for incessant innovation theologically and in modes of worship. Our need is for the perpetual renewing of the mind through the baptism of the Holy Spirit. Truth is progressively revealed. More treasures are yet to break forth from God's Word, but no heaven-sent message will ever subvert the force of already established truths. Each new truth adds luster and heightened relevance to the ancient treasure of established wisdom.

When we eat Christ's flesh and drink His blood, the element of eternal life will be found in the ministry. There will not be a fund of stale, oft-repeated ideas. The tame, dull sermonizing will cease. The old truths will be presented, but they will be seen in a new light. There will be a new perception of truth, a clearness and a power that all will discern. Those who have the privilege of sitting under such a ministry will, if susceptible to the Holy Spirit's influence, feel the energizing power of a new life. The fire of God's love will be kindled within them. Their perceptive faculties will be quickened to discern the beauty and majesty of truth. . . .

Springs of heavenly peace and joy, unsealed in the soul of the teacher by the words of Inspiration, will become a mighty river of influence to bless all who connect with him.[12]

Such a preacher of truth was John the Baptist. Such preachers and teachers may we also be!

In closing this section of our study, it would seem appropriate to consider two more points: Jesus' appraisal of John and John's death by martyrdom. Jesus spoke of John in the highest terms, contending that he was more than a prophet, that no person who ever lived was greater than John, and that he faithfully fulfilled his commission to restore all things (Matt. 11:7-11; 17:11-13). With a commendation like that from the Judge of all humankind, what detraction could one not endure from religious critics and worldlywise men! Jesus unequivocally identified John as the Elijah messenger prophesied in the book of Malachi (Matt. 11:12-15).

Christ also spoke of John's martyrdom in venerating terms, likening John's death as a foreshadowing of His own, thereby claiming fellowship with him in suffering (see Matt. 17:12, 13). John's death for the gospel's sake has for centuries sustained martyrs on their journey to the stake, the gallows, and the headsman's block, fortifying them for their final sacrifice in God's cause.

God never leads His children otherwise than they would choose to be led, if they could see the end from the beginning, and discern the glory of the purpose which they are fulfilling as coworkers with Him. Not Enoch who was translated to heaven, not Elijah, who ascended in a chariot of fire, was greater or more honored than John the Baptist, who perished alone in the dungeon. "Unto you it is given in the behalf of Christ, not only to believe on Him, but also to suffer for His sake." Phil. 1:29. And of all the gifts that Heaven can bestow upon men, fellowship with Christ in His sufferings is the most weighty trust and the highest honor.[13]

*Questions for Discussion and Reflection*

1. Identify and discuss at least three ways in which John's work as a restorer parallels the work God's last-day church is called on to perform as restorers.

2. What connection do you see between John's abstemious lifestyle and the Adventist Church's teachings on temperance and healthful living today? See *The Desire of Ages*, 101.

3. Identify two (or more) dangerous theological innovations that exist in our time and explain the dangers that accompany these ideas.

4. What can we learn from John the Baptist's life about how to keep the cross of Jesus central to our spiritual experience and beliefs?

---

1. Everyone recognizes that many Israelites were afflicted with an orthodox, works-based legalism (Rom. 9:30–10:4), but the idea that ancient Israel also had a liberal type of legalism may come as a surprise to some. Consider how God reproved His people for placing their faith in the presence of the ark among them as though it were a kind of rabbit's foot of security and divine protection whose power functioned on their behalf despite their living in flagrant idolatry and sin. See 1 Samuel 4:1-11. Samson had a legalistic faith in the protection that he would get from his long hair, feeling that he had license to give into his lowest passions and continue to enjoy divine favor if his locks remained unshorn. Legalism of both the conservative and liberal varieties is not merely a Jewish problem; it is a human problem and can be rooted out only by the power of the true gospel.

2. *Counsels to Parents, Teachers, and Students*, 445.

3. *Temperance*, 91. See also *Maranatha*, 62.

4. *This Day With God*, 217; cf.261.

5. *The Desire of Ages*, 219.

6. *Testimonies for the Church*, 4:338, 339.

7. *Review and Herald*, 22 April, 1909.

8. *Testimonies for the Church*, 8:333, 334.

9. *Gospel Workers*, 288, 289.

10. Ibid., 286, 287.

11. Ellen G. White Comments, *SDA Bible Commentary*, 7:958.

12. *Christ's Object Lessons*, 130-132.

13. *The Desire of Ages*, 224, 225.

# CHAPTER
# 17

# God's Third Elijah

London, February 26, 1791

Dear Sir—Unless the Divine power has raised you up [for the mission that drives you], I do not see how you can go through your glorious enterprise in opposing that execrable villainy, which is the scandal of religion, of England, and of human nature. Unless God has raised you up for this very thing, you will be worn out by the opposition of men and devils. But, "if God be for you, who can be against you?" Are all of them together stronger than God? . . . Go on in the name of God, and in the power of His might, till even American slavery shall vanish away before it."

Thus wrote John Wesley, four days before his death, to William Wilberforce, then an obscure member of the British Parliament. His letter was in reply to Wilberforce's appeal for counsel in his uphill battle against slavery and the slave trade. Only thirty-one years old, a member of the unpopular Methodist movement, and advocate of a cause whose opponents were rich and powerful, Wilberforce had a difficult mission. But the conviction burned within his heart that slavery in all its forms must be abolished. Wilberforce labored against the wind and tide of opposition for years before his determination led to a law to abolish slavery in England. The last phase of his proposed bills for the abolition of the slave trade gained parliamentary approval just three days before his death in 1833.

Wesley's words, adapted from Romans 8:31, "If God be for you, who can be against you?" rang true and inspired Wilberforce to persevere in his thankless task.

Elijah labored against similar opposition, only more intense. The abolition of Baal worship was hardly a celebrated cause in his day. And outside God's direct appointment and support, he had no open sponsorship for his great mission of reform. Likewise, John the Baptist did not enjoy the luxury of endorsement from the worldly great. He received no honorary degrees but rather was viewed as a dangerous heretic by the religious and political elite of Israel.

How is it, then, with God's last day Elijah people? Will the brokers of prestige rush to their door to decorate them with medals and ribbons of honor? Will Babylon express joyful commendation for the fearless candor of God's last day messengers? No more than Herod rewarded John the Baptist for his faithful witness. No more than Rome rewarded Paul for his glowing testimony. No more than Papal Rome applauded Martin Luther for his ninety-five theses.

It's precisely at this point, however, that we need to robustly withstand giving in to a martyr complex. If Wilberforce had spent his energies brooding over the massive opposition that confronted his crusade against slavery, he would have lost his courage and given up the struggle that eventually ended in triumph for his cause. If the heroes and heroines of faith throughout all ages had yielded to self-pity because of the scorn and ridicule that greeted their labors, they would have crept off the stage of action in shame, thus aborting the victory that God was preparing to grant in due season as a reward for their devotion.

God's faithful messengers, while they may weaken at times (as did Elijah, John the Baptist, Paul, Martin Luther, et al.), do not wallow in pessimistic despair. They do not dwell on their sufferings for His name's sake. Dismissing self-pity, they count the cost of discipleship and promptly pay it out of the bank of faith.

Self-centered people dwell on their sufferings and sacrifices, which usually exist more in their imagination than in reality. God-centered people draw strength and inspiration from the supreme sacrifice of Christ; they have little, if anything, to say about their great burdens and self-abandonment in a noble cause. They see themselves as unprofitable servants who, under the impulse of God's love, have only sought to do their duty (see Luke 17:10). And with Paul they can confidently declare, "I consider that the sufferings of this present time are not worthy to be compared with the glory which shall be revealed in us" (Rom. 8:18). It is significant that Hitler entitled his political testament *Mein Kampf* (My Struggle), whereas C. S. Lewis entitled his spiritual autobiography *Surprised by Joy*. The dictator envisioned himself as a great hero, a reformer of godlike proportions, while the Oxford don, in discovering the gospel that transformed his life, could only attest to the goodness and mercy of God in dealing with his proud, stony heart. From the time of his conversion to the close of his life, Lewis made it his business to recommend the grace of God to others. He had no time or inclination to comment on the mockery of those who despised his conversion to Christ, which was a shocking departure from the spiritually bankrupt intellectualism of his colleagues in the university where he taught.

Likewise, God's last-day Elijahs will not wallow in self-pity because their message is not widely appreciated. They will not snivel because somebody frowned at their words or threatened their lives. Nor will they lash out with vexation against their opponents. Intrepid, yet tactful, they will bear their God-given message, let the consequences be what they will. They will not bemoan their unpopularity. This consideration is important. "This is no time for the people of God to be weaklings."[1] We must put on the whole armor of God and press forward with our task of proclaiming the true gospel to the world—the gospel that renovates lives and demolishes error.

But it's not realistic or healthy to romanticize the faith of God's true heroes. Elijah panicked when Jezebel threatened his life; John the Baptist had doubts about Jesus' messiahship while languishing in prison, Paul wavered in the face of his long, arduous journey to Rome, until taking fresh heart when he saw his converts assemble along the Appian Way; Martin Luther faltered on the eve of the Diet of Worms until fortified by a friend's encouraging words. God's true witnesses all have their moments of weakness and doubt, but they do not wallow in this element and dwell in Doubting Castle as their final abode. They do not make fear and hesitation a staple of their diet. Rather, they go on from faith to faith, from strength to strength, from glory to glory, in the pursuit of their divinely charted course.

God's perfect love casts out all fear, not while we wait for all fogs to lift and all obstacles to be cleared from our pathway but while we press on in the face of often stupendous challenges, relying not on our own strength and ingenuity but on His promises and protection.

During England's final campaign against Napoleon, the Duke of Wellington sent two lieutenants on horseback through enemy-held territory to deliver an important message to another division of English troops. Both men carried the same coded message in case only one got through enemy lines. As they galloped along for several miles in pursuit of their dangerous mission, one of the lieutenants looked at his colleague. Observing his blanched face and trembling chin, the officer indignantly cried out, "Why, man, are you *afraid*?" "Y-y-yes," replied his colleague. Immediately the other officer wheeled his horse about and galloped back to Wellington's tent. Bursting into the general's presence, he declared, "Sir, I will not ride with a coward." Wellington asked, "Did your brother officer ride on in the direction I ordered you both to go?" "Well, sir, yes." "Then you had better remount your horse and hasten on, or the coward will have the business done before you overtake him."

For the child of God in the midst of troublous times, fightings may be without and fears within, but as we press on in the direction our Savior bids us go, we shall gain mastery of our fears. Our courage will rise as we perform our duty, trusting in God to see us through. "Whenever I am afraid I will trust in You" (Ps. 56:3).

Who then is God's third Elijah? It is those spoken of in Malachi 4:5, 6 who serve as Christ's forerunners to proclaim His second appearing and call on people everywhere to prepare to meet the Lord. In Revelation 14:1-12 we discover that these witnesses are the 144,000. See this thought developed in *Manuscript Releases*, volume 18, pages 27-29, and compare with Revelation 7:1-14.[2]

The most fascinating distinction about this final group of witnesses is not their number (as to whether it is literal or figurative); it is their character and experience, all of which centers on intense love and loyalty to Jesus. They not only behold the Lamb of God with the eye of faith but also follow Him wherever He leads. His itinerary with His people takes them to earth's remotest regions, to homes over which suffering and poverty cling like a shroud, to palaces and prisons, to courts and colleges, to jungles and geriatric wards—to all places where people are, people who need to hear the gospel and see its power exemplified in converted lives. His faithful witnesses cheerfully endure scorn, privations, and persecution in serving with their Lord.

What special resource do the 144,000 draw on to bravely carry out their demanding and dangerous mission? It is God's love, whose perfect manifestation in the lives of His truly committed people casts out all fear (see 1 John 4:18). He makes them loyal in His cause, fearless in doing His will, loving in their motives, and intensely evangelistic.

> The Lord has a people on the earth, who follow the Lamb whithersoever He goeth. He has His thousands who have not bowed the knee to Baal. Such will stand with Him on Mount Zion. But they must stand on this earth, girded with the whole armor, ready to engage in the work of saving those who are ready to perish. Heavenly angels conduct this search, and spiritual activity is demanded of all who believe present truth, that they may join the angels in their work.[3]

The character and work of the 144,000 corresponds closely to that of John the Baptist. It is this correlation that makes the study of John the Baptist so relevant.

> In this age, just prior to the second coming of Christ in the clouds of heaven, such a work as that of John is to be done. God calls for men who will prepare a people to stand in the great day of the Lord. The message preceding the public ministry of Christ was . . . "repent ye; for the kingdom of heaven is at hand." As a people who believe in Christ's

soon appearing, we have a message to bear—"Prepare to meet thy God." Amos 4:12. Our message must be as direct as was the message of John. He rebuked kings for their iniquity. Notwithstanding that his life was imperiled, he did not hesitate to declare God's word. And our work in this age must be done as faithfully.

In order to give such a message as John gave, we must have a spiritual experience like his. The same work must be wrought in us. We must behold God, and in beholding Him lose sight of self.[4]

Please note the above paragraph carefully. If we attempt to be like John the Baptist in denouncing sin but fail to partake of the divine nature through lack of intimacy with Christ, we shall offer nothing but an abrasive, vitriolic caricature of John. We shall misrepresent reform and make it seem spiteful, censorious, and repellent. Instead of having humility and self-abasement as did John, we shall have a steel-plated self-righteousness, impervious to reason and conciliation. This is counterfeit reform.

When we study the Bible's picture of the 144,000, we discover a people who are entirely free from falseness and extremism. Extraordinary, yes, but not extreme. While not all questions can be answered this side of Paradise concerning the 144,000, we should aspire to be part of this group for the glory of God and the advancement of His cause.

Let us strive with all the power that God has given us to be among the hundred and forty-four thousand. And let us do all that we can to help others to gain heaven. We are to have an intense interest in Christ Jesus; for he is our Saviour. He came to this world to be tempted in all points as we are, to prove to the universe that in this world of sin human beings can live lives that God will approve.[5]

Carefully read the Bible's description of this elect group in Revelation 7:1-4 and 14:1-5. These are the people who are sealed and commissioned to give the third angel's message in its ever expanding relevance and power. And we have this assurance: "Large numbers will be admitted who in these last days hear the truth for the first time."[6]

Based on the passages just cited, let's look at the chief characteristics of the 144,000.
• They have not defiled themselves with women, but are virgins.[7]
• They are citizens of the true Israel of God.[8]
• They follow the Lamb wherever He goes.
• They have been redeemed from mankind.
• In their mouth there is no lie.
• They are without fault before God's throne.
• They bear the seal of the living God.

Their experience may be summarized by Paul's testimony to the Philippians: "For to me, to live is Christ" (Phil. 1:21). Thoroughly rooted in the gospel, they are vibrantly motivated to share with others the truth that has brought such abundant benefit to their own lives. As human messengers intimately leagued with heaven for the proclamation of present truth, they cannot bottle up the joy of salvation or speak of it in hushed, apologetic tones. With heaven-born tact and zeal they proclaim a crucified and risen Savior to the world.[9] They exemplify in their lives the full benefits of receiving the everlasting gospel as "the power of God to salvation" (Rom. 1:16). In thought, word, and deed they mirror the light of the message they bear. And because their lives demonstrate what they preach, their message has credibility and appeal. Having drunk of Christ, the fountain of truth and life, rivers of living water flow from them too (see John 7:37-39). As recipients of the latter rain, they are conduits for its outward flow toward others. They operate in the power of God's final Pentecost.

The message they declare exalts Christ and His righteousness as revealed in His life and law. This revelation brings repentance, victory, refreshment, and joy to the hearts of all who welcome the word of life. Those who joyfully receive Christ and His Word are given power to overcome all evil, and they have faith to do exploits in God's name (see 1 John 2:14; Heb. 11:35-40). Many of those who hear and see the 144,000 catch the vision and discover for themselves that "through faith in Christ, every deficiency of character may be supplied, every defilement cleansed, every fault corrected, every excellence developed."[10] And they fully commit themselves to this experience, too, which has already been developing in their lives through the work of the Holy Spirit on their hearts.

As commandment keepers, whose whole loyalty and affections are centered in Christ, the 144,000 provoke the devil's fury. This is especially so, because God has empowered them to be agents in liberating multitudes from Satan's deceptions and control. They are a wakeful, illuminated people whose love for God translates itself into devoted obedience to His teachings and laws. Their minds are inquiring but not doubtful. Their conversation is in heaven, from whence they look for their Savior (Phil. 3:20). They purify themselves in the saving mercies of the Lamb (Rev. 7:13, 14), and have confidence in the power of His grace, by which they are preparing for translation into His kingdom.

At the same time they have no boastful claims to make about their righteousness or salvation. All their praise and thanksgiving goes to God. So closely are they united to their Lord that without presumption or pretense they can declare with the psalmist, "Because your lovingkindness is better than life, my lips shall praise You" (Ps. 63:3). It is this spirit of self-transcendent devotion that enables the 144,000 to rise above the fear of the death decree and courageously declare God's Word at the peril of their lives (Rev. 13:15-17; 14:9-12). The glory of God and the salvation of others is more important to them than escape from suffering and death. Ever sustained and inspired by the memory of Christ's sufferings and sacrifice, they persevere in their mission for Christ. Like the apostle Paul, they are "appointed for the defense of the gospel" (Phil. 1:17). Like Elijah and John the Baptist before them, the 144,000 are driven by a zeal for God's glory. And that zeal takes the twofold form of seeking to be like Jesus and to turn as many as possible to Him, all for His glory and not their own. This is true fruit bearing. For this very work, God's people are richly endowed with the Holy Spirit, that Christ might minister through their witness.

When the apostles were filled with the Holy Spirit, their

hearts were surcharged with a benevolence so full, so deep, so far-reaching, that it impelled them to go to the ends of the earth, testifying to the power of Christ. They were filled with an intense longing to carry forward the work He had begun. They realized the greatness of their debt to heaven and the responsibility of their work. Strengthened by the endowment of the Holy Spirit, they went forth filled with zeal to extend the triumphs of the cross.[11]

In God's last day witnesses the gospel will produce the same consecration, enthusiasm, and divine energy to witness as it did in those who received the Holy Spirit at Pentecost. In fact, the power and inspiration that will animate God's people in the last days will surpass the experience of the apostolic church. "The outpouring of the Spirit in the days of the apostles was the former rain, and glorious was the result. But the latter rain will be more abundant."[12] Why? It needs to be greater for at least three reasons. *First*, this is the final warning message that *the world* shall hear. When it ends, no more message of mercy will be given; probation will conclude, and Christ will come to gather in the harvest ripened by the latter rain. *Second*, at the close of time Satan is working with unprecedented power to deceive and unbridled fury to destroy; the latter rain forcefully counteracts this strong current of evil. *Third*, the human population and the diversity of its beliefs have never been so great; the latter rain is needed to surmount these vast challenges and cause the truth to shine forth with matchless clarity and splendor. God has decreed that by the light of the three angels He will lighten the earth with His glory and thus effect a complete deliverance of all His people from Babylon (Rev. 18:1-5). It is to achieve this vital result that He sends the latter rain.

As they proclaim the third angel's message, the 144,000 never lose sight that for all its imperative warning content, this message is the everlasting *gospel* and not a mere apocalyptic tirade with which to assail the world. "As the third angel's message swells into a loud cry, great power and glory will attend its proclamation. The faces of God's people will shine with the light of heaven."[13] With the purity, joy, and vitality of true godliness they make the last gospel appeal to a frantic, frightened, groping world. Many people will hear the echo of the true Shepherd's voice in this proclamation and with thankful haste will come out of Babylon to join the remnant church, which keeps the commandments of God and has the faith of Jesus.

Thus the 144,000 are God's beacons to illuminate the world with Christ's righteousness. They bear this sacred privilege not because they have become great in their own eyes or emboldened by a sense of their own holiness but because Christ is all and in all to them. Self is eclipsed in the radiance of His grace and glory. Raptly they have beheld the Lamb, and briskly they have followed His steps in carrying out their appointed mission of mercy. They are not preoccupied with their saintliness but with His saving goodness, thus clearing the way for Christ to fulfill in them the work of faith with power and fruitfulness. He alone is exalted to them—and through them. Sealed with His character, they and all who have left Babylon in response to heaven's warning are ready for Christ's return.

*Questions for Discussion and Reflection*

1. Summarize the character description of the 144,000 that is given in Revelation 14:3-5.

2. How do the 144,000 develop characters that receive God's unqualified approval?

3. What does it mean to you to "follow the Lamb wherever He goes"?

4. What gives special power to the message of the 144,000? Why does their message contain a strong warning element, along with a richly appealing proclamation of Christ and His righteousness?

---

1. *Testimonies for the Church*, 8:42.

2. For additional evidence of the evangelistic activity and fruitfulness of the 144,000,

consider this description of them. "We all entered the cloud together, and were seven days ascending to the sea of glass, when Jesus brought the crowns, and with His own right hand placed them on our heads. He gave us harps of gold and palms of victory. Here on the sea of glass the 144,000 stood in a perfect square. Some of them had very bright crowns, others not so bright. Some crowns appeared heavy with stars, while others had but few" *(Early Writings,* 16).

Now consider the interpretation of the star-studded crowns: "In their crowns of rejoicing those who are rescued by them and finally saved will shine as stars forever and ever" (Ibid., 61). For Scripture substantiation of this symbol, see Isa. 62:3; Dan. 12:3; Zech. 9:16; 1 Thess. 2:19. Inasmuch, then, as the 144,000 are given star-laden crowns, we may conclude that they have been productive soul winners, conveying God's last message of warning and mercy to the world. Hence the association of the 144,000 with the three angels' messages in Rev. 14:1-12. Their experience has been shaped by the messages, and they proclaim them from the vantage point of a personal experience of the power enfolded in this final proclamation of the everlasting gospel.

3. Ellen G. White Comments, *SDA Bible Commentary,* 7:798.

4. Ibid., 332, 333.

5. *Review and Herald,* 9 March 1905.

6. *Review and Herald,* 5 July 1906.

7. This is a symbolic reference to their having departed from the churches of Babylon, which teach false doctrine and misrepresent God's character by an alliance with civil power to violently enforce false doctrine and corrupt worship (see Revelation 17:1-5).

8. This does not mean that the 144,000 are all literal Jews, although Jewish converts will undoubtedly be among them. The 144,000 are spiritual Israel from every nation, kindred, tongue, and people (see Ps. 73:1; Rom. 2:28, 29; 9:6; 10:12; Phil. 3:3).

9. They have no desire to make trouble or humiliate Babylon. It is simply their irrepressible determination to exalt Christ and lead others to Him in a saving way. But in the process of doing this, they find themselves constrained by the Spirit to pronounce the fall of Babylon and warn God's true people to come out of her communion. "In every generation God has sent His servants to rebuke sin, both in the world and in the church. But the people desire smooth things to be spoken to them, and the pure, unvarnished truth is not acceptable. Many reformers, in entering upon their work, determined to exercise great prudence in attacking the sins of the church and the nation. They hoped by the example of a pure Christian life, to lead the people back to the doctrines of the Bible. But the Spirit of God came upon them as it came upon Elijah, moving him to rebuke the sins of a wicked king and an apostate people; they could not refrain from preaching the utterances of the Bible—doctrines which they had been reluctant to present. They were impelled to zealously declare the truth and the danger which threatened souls. The words which the Lord gave them they uttered, fearless of consequences, and the people were compelled to hear the warning" *(The Great Controversy,* 606).

We note that it is not generally men and women of fiery temperament whom the Lord chooses to lead in a work of reform. Some people gleefully relish the role of the iconoclast, the exploder of tradition, the smasher of heresies. And they vigorously assert their own ideas as the true voice of God. Such are too egocentric and belligerent to qualify as genuine reformers. They do not have God's glory in view but their own.

10. *Education*, 257. The 144,000 recognize that the power to live a victorious Christian life is just as much an act of *unmerited favor* from God as forgiveness from sin. They do not see victory as their contribution to the salvation process but as the manifestation of Christ's glory and free grace flowing through their lives. They have the unified fourfold experience described in 1 Corinthians 1:30 of finding in Christ their wisdom, righteousness, sanctification, and redemption, that all their glory may be in the Lord and in Him alone (see 1 Cor. 1:31).

11. *The Acts of the Apostles*, 46.

12. *Evangelism*, 701.

13. *Testimonies for the Church*, 7:17.

# CHAPTER
# 18

# Laodicea, a Restored, Victorious Church

As we have seen, John's work, according to Jesus, was to *restore* all things. This is also the work of God's last-day Elijah, the 144,000. In the Greek of the gospel writers, *restore* means to "bring back to a former condition of health." The same Greek word (*apokathistemi*) is found in a passage that describes Christ's healing of a man's withered hand. In obedience to Christ's command, the afflicted man stretched forth his hand, "and it was restored whole, like as the other" (Matt. 12:13).

The spiritual implication of the word *restore* in reference to John's ministry is that God was overseeing a restoration and renewal of Israel's broken and distorted covenant relations with Him, a healing of their deep spiritual wounds, inflicted by Satan. This healing involved a restoration of the people's understanding and appreciation of pure Bible truth. John's grasp of the essence of God's covenant with Israel led him to proclaim Jesus as the Lamb of God, who takes away the sin of the world. His central aim was to point people to this Lamb and encourage them to become attached to Him. This was the direct avenue to restoration for all who accepted the message. John's work was to help the people of his day to accept Jesus as the Savior, the only One who could restore their souls.

John's mission reveals the essential work of God's last day Elijah movement. Jesus is coming. He wants us to be ready for that event. Without the right kind of preparation that restores our souls, by imparting to us the truth in all its intrinsic power and worth, Christ's second coming will ring in the day of our doom rather than deliverance.

Only a restored people can effectively deliver a message of restoration. Unless the truth we attempt to proclaim grips, transforms, and vitalizes our own lives, it will seem like a falsehood to those who hear us. Like a parable in the mouth of a fool, the message of present truth will come out tortured and twisted unless it has transformed our lives. Contrast Proverbs 26:7, 9 with Luke 3:4, 5. The Lord wishes for us to become living epistles—embodiments of His Word and examples of His character. Only thus can we be restorers of paths to dwell in.

But in Revelation Christ discloses that the very people appointed to carry out this mission are alarmingly unfit for it. He speaks to the church in the closing age, the one in which the Elijah message is to be consummated, words of special warning, reproof, counsel, and appeal. He also speaks encouragement to those who heed Him (see Christ's epistle to Laodicea, Rev. 3:14-22).

In this chapter we will take a quick overview of that epistle in its practical bearings. We will especially focus on the rich gospel content of the message to Laodicea. After all, whatever Christ says to His people is always the gospel in one or more of its aspects. At least this is true while the door of hope is open, as it is to Laodicea. In connection with this overview, we will see how Christ's message to Laodicea is designed to prepare us for being overcomers, fully equipped for our mission as God's last-day witnesses.

Let's read His message to Laodicea.

And to the angel of the church of the Laodiceans write, "These things says the Amen, the Faithful and True Witness, the Beginning of the creation of God: I know your works, that you are neither cold nor hot. I could wish you were cold or hot. So then, because you are lukewarm, and neither cold nor hot, I will spew you out of My mouth. Because you say, 'I am rich, have become wealthy, and have need of nothing'—and do not know that you are wretched, miserable, poor, blind, and naked—I counsel you to buy from Me gold refined in the fire, that you may be rich; and white garments, that you may be clothed, that the shame of your nakedness may not be revealed; and anoint your eyes with eye salve, that you may see. As many as I love, I rebuke and chasten. Therefore be zealous and repent. Behold, I stand at the door and knock. If anyone hears My voice and opens the door, I will come in to him and dine with him, and he with Me. To him who overcomes I will grant to sit with Me on My throne, as I also overcame and sat down with My Father on His throne. He who has an ear, let him hear what the Spirit says to the churches " (Rev. 3:14-22).

Christ, the great Physician, and the true Witness to Laodicea, unerringly diagnoses His church's condition. He sees His professed people in the depths of complacent backsliddenness that would be altogether fatal except for the miraculous cure that He offers.

Some church members shun discussing the Laodicean message, because they feel that it is a message of condemnation, offering little, if any, hope. Their feelings may be based on the way the message is sometimes explained. But it would be a serious mistake to turn away from the message, for it is sent from the heart of Christ to His last-day church. "The warning for the last church . . . must be proclaimed to all who claim to be Christians. The Laodicean message, like a sharp, two-edged sword must go to all the churches."[1] How important, then, that we grasp the true import of this message and recognize the redemptive spirit in which it is sent. The message is a surgical tool, not a slaughter weapon. It is meant to bring us all to humble, heart-searching prayer, rather than to angry contempt for the church. Christ's message to Laodicea is not "Abandon the church" but "Abandon sloth and self-righteousness; make your calling and election sure in Me."

We will have a better appreciation of the whole message if we consider the meaning of the word *Laodicea*. Laodicea means *a people under judgment*. This points to the time of the message.

Many students of Bible prophecy know from Daniel 8:13, 14; 9:24-27 that God's judgment began in 1844. So the very name of this church points to the era it represents. As the seventh and last phase of church history, the Laodicean period began in 1844 and extends to the close of time.

Judgment time may sound unnerving. It may seem to suddenly raise questions and doubts about one's security in Christ. But Christ pointed out that many go through their religious lives with a solid assurance for which they have no warrant (Matt. 7:21-23; 24:36-51). He spoke of this false assurance in several parables (e.g., Matt. 22:1-13; Matt. 25:1-46). Jesus certainly wants us to have assurance, but assurance of the right kind, based on the solid verities of His gospel which, when fully accepted, bring about a life-transforming connection with Him. God's judgment is not designed to rob us of assurance in Christ and His salvation.

At the same time, however, the reality of God's judgment, and the proclamation that it is now in progress, definitely should shake us loose from the Laodicean self-assurance that we are in top form spiritually when in reality we are wretched, miserable, poor, blind, and naked. How absurd to maintain and promote assurance under such conditions as these! Gospel assurance is not equivalent to prideful self-satisfaction that nothing can disturb. Rather, the "full assurance of faith" comes to those whose hearts are surrendered to Christ and purified from sin (see Heb. 6:11, 12; 10:22).

John Newton, author of the hymn "Amazing Grace", wrote, "I would not give one straw for that assurance that sin will not damp. If David had come to me in his adultery and had talked to me of his assurance, I would have despised his speech."[2] But after David's repentance, the Lord restored to him the joy of salvation. Read Psalm 51.

Paul received much assurance from the thought of God's judgment. He expresses it thus: "'Truly, these times of ignorance God overlooked, but now commands all men everywhere to repent, because He has appointed a day on which He will judge the world in righteousness by the Man whom He has ordained. He has given assurance of this to all by raising Him from the dead'" (Acts 17:30, 31).

God's time of judgment is one in which each professed follower of Christ will be either condemned or justified (vindicated), depending on each individual's response to the gospel. It is true that we are *justified* in Christ the very moment we accept Him as Savior (Rom. 3:24-28, 30). Christ's *judgment* serves to demonstrate whether we have continued in His grace, and welcomed the gospel as the ruling power of our lives, or have simply tried to exploit the gospel as an excuse for living in selfishness and sin while claiming the honor of being born-again children of God. Paul made this clear in his letter to the confused believers in Galatia: "'But if, while we seek to be justified by Christ, we ourselves also are found sinners, is Christ therefore a minister of sin? Certainly not!'" (Gal. 2:17). "Therefore consider the goodness and severity of God: on those who fell, severity; but toward you, goodness, if you continue in His goodness. Otherwise you also will be cut off" (Rom. 11:22).

God's judgment exhibits the results of His saving work in the life of each professed Christian. Those who abide in Him, assimilating His life and truth, are shown in the judgment as cleansed, purified, ennobled by the gospel, partakers of the divine nature. Their record of spiritual beautification serves to vindicate the gospel, proving that it possesses the power to make sinners every whit whole in Christ. Those who are condemned in the judgment meet this fate because, while they happily take Christ's name, they have rejected the character-transforming work of His grace in their lives. They are not partakers of the divine nature, as they would easily have been, had they really welcomed the enthronement of Christ in their hearts.

God announces His judgment, not to chill our hopes or thrust us into despair but to awaken us to our true condition and need, so that we might make Him our sufficiency. "When we are judged, we are chastened by the Lord, *that we may not be condemned with the world*" (1 Cor. 11:32). I would far rather be told of my sins and shortcomings now, while they can be remedied through Christ's power, than after it is too late, and I am hopelessly lost. Wouldn't you? "For we have become partakers of Christ if we hold the beginning of our confidence steadfast to the end, while it is said: 'Today, if you will hear His voice, do not harden your hearts as in the rebellion'" (Heb. 3:14, 15).

Viewed in the light of its being an opportunity to make our calling and election sure, the judgment emerges, at least for the redeemed, as a betrothal process rather than as a strain in their relations with God, or a cause of estrangement from Him. The judgment is not a divorce proceeding but a marriage for those who unite with Christ in heart and mind. It is a ratification and full exhibition of Christ's effectual work in the lives of the redeemed.

One can view the judgment as a stern checking-up process or as a time of friendly disclosure in which the plan of salvation is fully validated and vindicated by a detailed examination of its wonderful results in the lives of all who fully accept Jesus. In addition, the Lord clears His faithful people of all the false charges brought against them by Satan and his earthly cohorts. After all, in the history of Christendom God's people have often been accused of heresy and crimes of which they were totally innocent—their only "guilt" being that of faithfulness to unpopular truth. For these the judgment is a time of glorious vindication. "For the Lord will not cast off His people, nor will He forsake His inheritance. But judgment will return to righteousness, and all the upright in heart will follow it" (Ps. 94:14, 15).

If our lives are mired in unvictorious living, then the judgment message terrifies rather than cheers us. Christ's counsel to Laodicea, however, is a lifeline extended to draw us out of the morass of defeat and despair and place us securely on the road to victory in Him.

His very introduction of Himself to Laodicea is given to inspire confidence in Jesus. He is the "Amen," the one whose counsel is clear and reliable, whose authority is solid, and whose purposes are stable. He teaches us to rise above the spirit of frothy modernism that tries to make all truth "relative" and subject to constant revision with the "progress" of human thought. "His truth endures to all generations" (Ps. 100:5).

As the faithful and true witness, Jesus highlights His role in the judgment as the One who has a perfect knowledge of our lives and who speaks only truth that none can refute, not even Satan.

At the beginning (i.e., source, "*arche*," in Greek) of the creation of God, Jesus declares His creatorship (compare Rev. 3:14 with

Rev. 14:7). This pertinent characterization not only anticipates and overturns the theory of evolution that has predominated modern thought for the past six generations, it also emphasizes Christ's ability, as Creator, to make any needed change in our lives. His power and authority are supreme. And His willingness to exercise that power for us beneficially is absolute.

But He speaks to a people who, while having access to all truth and spiritual power, are living in the depths of spiritual poverty. Why this unnecessary dearth? "Here is a people who pride themselves in their possession of spiritual knowledge and advantages. But they have not responded to the unmerited blessings that God has bestowed upon them."[3]

Because most Laodiceans haven't really appropriated the benefits of the gospel and are largely unacquainted with the Savior, their experience lacks fervor and focus. They are unable to be a light to the world at the very time the Lord wants them to radiate the brilliance of His truth and love. They are sleeping watchers rather than wakeful guides. We are Laodicea. Ellen White wrote, "The message to the Laodicean church reveals our condition as a people."[4]

Despite Laodicea's deeply entrenched complacency and stupefying self-righteousness, Jesus does not look upon our case as hopeless.[5] Because Laodicea's condition is remediable, He offers counsel. It comes in three parts, which all combine into one experience. Jesus depicts Himself as a heavenly Merchantman going from house to house to sell three priceless wares:

1. *Gold tried in the fire.* From 1 Peter 1:7 we discover that the gold refined in fire represents an active faith, one that works by love (Gal. 5:6). This faith purifies the heart that unreservedly surrenders to Christ and welcomes His offered righteousness (see Acts 15:9; Phil. 3:9). Faith is not self-existent or self-perpetuating; Jesus is the Author and Finisher of our faith. Our faith will grow stronger and purer as we immerse it in the cleansing fire of His Word and live it out in the crucible of life's experience (Jer. 23:29; James 1:3; 2 Cor. 4:17, 18).

2. *White raiment.* Spiritual nakedness is the result of sin. The loss of their garment of light was Adam and Eve's first palpable

evidence that their disobedience to God had made a change in their lives. Immediately they tried to compensate for their nakedness by making aprons of fig leaves. They could cover their physical nudity in part but could devise nothing to take the place of the divine righteousness they had so rashly forfeited.

Through the gospel, Christ offers to end forever our spiritual nakedness by placing upon us the rich robe of His own eternal righteousness. This righteousness is not just an outward covering but an inweaving of the attributes of Christ's nature into our character. By grace, divine righteousness becomes integral to our essential being. Thus Christ's robe of fine linen is the "righteousness of saints" (Rev. 19:7, 8). Not righteousness the saints generate, accumulate, or humanly cultivate but righteousness that is imputed and imparted to them as a divine gift. It is "the righteousness of God, through Jesus Christ to all and on all who believe. For there is no difference" (Rom. 3:22). Christ will not ascribe a righteousness to us that we have not received and incorporated into our lives.

3. *Eye salve.* Symbolically, eye salve represents the power of clear discernment that only the Holy Spirit can give us. God imparts His Spirit to all who willingly respond to the overtures of His love. That willing response expresses itself in the desire to know, love, and serve Jesus in a constantly deeper and richer way.

Jesus was anointed with the Spirit and with power at His baptism (Acts 10:38). This same Spirit anoints us with power to live and serve as Jesus did when we make ourselves submissive to the Spirit's authority, as Jesus did. When this attitude is ours, then Paul's prayer for the believers in Ephesus will also be fulfilled to us: "That the God of our Lord Jesus Christ, the Father of glory, may give to you the spirit of wisdom and revelation in the knowledge of Him, the eyes of your understanding being enlightened; that you may know what is the hope of His calling, what are the riches of the glory of His inheritance in the saints, and what is the exceeding greatness of His power toward us who believe, according to the working of His mighty power which He worked in Christ when He raised Him from the dead and seated Him at His right hand in the heavenly places" (Eph. 1:17-20). Such an anointed vision of life will keep us from spiritual snares, stagnation, and sloth. Backsliding will be impossible and vital progress sure. We will enjoy a deep intimacy with God. Scripture reading will be a personal interview with a living God, rather than a mere perusal of revered testimonies by ancient writers.

"The 'eyesalve,' the Word of God, makes the conscience smart under its application, for it convicts of sin. But the smarting is necessary that the healing may follow, and the eye be single to the glory of God."[6]

To have anointed eyes is to view life from God's perspective. It is to see people as He sees them, to interpret the events of life as He does. It is to hold Him in supreme regard. I shall never forget the lesson I learned on the *true art of seeing*. It was from a fellow Christian who was physically blind. Grace Jajeh lost her vision during her childhood in Lebanon. She came to the United States with her parents as a refugee. I knew her while she was a student at the Lighthouse for the Blind in San Francisco, where I worked in the office of education as a clerk. During her youth Grace became a Christian. Naturally she longed to have her eyesight back and knew that in her glorified body, given at Jesus' coming, she would once more be able to see. But at times she was depressed by her blindness and the limitations this handicap imposed on her. One night she had a dream in which an angel asked her, "If you could have your choice between two blessings—the return of your eyesight in this life, or the privilege of winning a soul for Jesus, which would you choose?"

When Grace told us her dream the next morning in the front office at the Lighthouse, she beamed ecstatically and said, "I awoke shouting, 'A soul for Jesus, a soul for Jesus!' "

Though her physical eyes were blind, Grace had truly anointed spiritual vision. Her testimony that morning consolidated my determination to live for Jesus without faintheartedness or compromise. I can only imagine that it had a similar effect on the others who heard her.

Those who hunger and thirst for God's companionship, who long to hear His voice speaking through His Word, and wish to see His reflection in all His creation are the ones who anoint their eyes with eye salve that they may see. They welcome the Spirit's fellowship and work in their lives because it is His office to reveal Christ and bring His Word to life in our experience (John 14:15, 16, 26). They cheerfully obey God, not to earn salvation or favor but because through Calvary they have already found His favor and now enjoy doing those things that please Him. In the process, they discover that doing His will becomes also their own highest pleasure.

Christ yearns for us to have this experience. He labors to arouse us to a sense of His desire for us and our need for Him. That's why He declares, "'As many as I love, I rebuke and chasten. Therefore be zealous and repent'" (Rev. 3:19). He would not invite us to repent unless we had the prospect of becoming converted through His grace. As with the church at Corinth, it is our privilege to zealously repent, and, through the righteousness of Christ, occupy a position of uncompromised favor with Him (see 2 Cor. 7:8-12).

"The counsel of the true Witness is full of encouragement and comfort. The churches may yet obtain the gold of truth, faith, and love, and be rich in heavenly treasure."[7]

"But these precious treasures will not drop upon us without some exertion on our part. We must buy—we must be 'zealous and repent' of our lukewarm state. We must be awake to see our wrongs, to search for our sins, and to put them away from us."[8] We can accomplish this only through Christ, our righteousness. It is the worthiness of Christ that must save us, His blood that must cleanse us. If we cast away our pride and wash our robes in the blood of the Lamb, then His counsel will take full, soul-saving effect in our lives. We will then be fitted to shine as lights in the world and proclaim the three angels' messages in the full power of the Holy Spirit. But unless we heed the counsel of the True Witness to Laodicea, what gospel message do we have to bring to anyone? That of a Savior whom we do not know, whose voice and knock we hear but do not answer?

Jesus stands at our heart's door knocking, not with thunderous insistence but with the still small voice of loving entreaty for entrance into our lives. When we let Him in, He feeds us with the hidden manna of truth, with the bread of His own being, thereby making us partakers of the divine nature. He imparts to us the satisfaction and empowerment of His holy love, through the Spirit residing in us and presiding over our joyfully yielded hearts. This is soul-nourishment indeed and friendship from One who sticks closer than a brother.

He gives us victory by the freely offered means of His Word, His Spirit, and His blood (Rev. 12:11). And then, wonder of supernal wonders—He offers us a place with Him on His throne, the throne to which we often resorted as a place of refuge and instruction, the throne of mercy and judgment before which we have contritely appeared, confessing our sins, seeking His grace to live pure, godly lives, according to His commandment and promise (Matt. 5:24, 48; 1 Thess. 5:23, 24; 1 Tim. 5:24).[9]

Christ's message to Laodicea, while unsparing in its diagnosis of our sins and as direct as the messages of Elijah and John the Baptist to God's professed people, is full of promise and hope to Laodiceans who repent and accept His threefold counsel to His church. It is our privilege to have indomitable faith, incorruptible righteousness, and inextinguishable vision through the power of an indwelling Christ. May we promptly accept these gifts to Laodicea with contrition, gratitude, and praise.

## Questions for Discussion and Reflection

1. Why is it wrong to make Christ's message to Laodicea a vehicle of condemnation to other believers or to the church? See 1 Cor. 11:32 in connection with Rev. 3:19 and Ps. 92:12-14; *Selected Messages*, 2:68, 69.

2. What connection exists between Christ's promise to Laodicea and the present truth on the sanctuary that has been committed to the Laodicean church? See Rev. 3:21; Heb. 4:14-16; 6:17-20; 10:12-23. See also *The Great Controversy*, 423, 488-490.

3. Someone says to you, "I'm leaving the Laodicean church; it's too backslidden. I'm going to join the invisible church of Philadelphia, which has the true Spirit of God." How would you advise this person and show him his error from the Bible? Consider the counsel and promises to Laodicea (Rev. 3:19-21; cf. James 5:9-11; Luke 12:36-40).

4. Have you heard Christ knocking on your heart's door and let Him in?

---

1. *Testimonies for the Church*, 6:77.

2. John Newton in *Illustrative Gatherings*, Second Series, G. S. Bowes, editor (London: James Nisbet and Co., 1865), 14.

3. *Selected Messages*, 1:357.

4. *Review and Herald*, 15 December 1904.

5. "The design of the message to the Laodiceans was to rid the church of . . . fanatical influences; but the effort of Satan has been to corrupt the message, and destroy its influence. He would be better pleased to have fanatical persons embrace the testimony, and use it in his cause, than to have them remain in a lukewarm state. I have seen that it was not the design of the message to lead brother to sit in judgment over his brother, to tell him what to do, and just how far to go, but for each individual to search his own heart, and attend to his own individual work" (Ellen G. White Comments, *SDA Bible Commentary*, 7:962).

6. *Our High Calling*, 350.

7. Ellen G. White Comments, *SDA Bible Commentary*, 7:965.

8. *Our High Calling*, 351.

9. "We can overcome. Yes, fully, entirely. Jesus died to make a way of escape for us, that we might overcome every fault, resist every temptation, and sit down at last with Him on His throne" (*Our High Calling*, 353).

# CHAPTER
# 19

# The Message and Mission of the 144,000

**W**hile on her way to work one spring morning in 1962, my mother awaited her turn to cross a busy intersection in Brooklyn. Stepping off the curb when the traffic light turned in her favor, she heard a man across the street shout, "Step back—NOW!" Instinctively, my mother and those crossing with her retreated under the scaffolding that covered the sidewalk. A second later several pieces of slate tile shattered at their feet. Had the pedestrians ignored the stranger's warning, some of them would have been seriously injured, perhaps even killed by the heavy tiling that fell from high overhead. But they responded swiftly to his sharp command, not politely worded, not sounded in tender tones, but certainly prompted by honest concern for the safety of people unaware of their peril. None of them took offense for being shouted at. Their immediate danger required an urgent warning and direct order. And so it is sometimes with God's messages to us, especially when the situation is critical and time is short.[1]

Intense, taut, urgent, God's final message to the world commands full attention and quick response. Able communicators give a message that meets the need and nature of their audience. God knows His audience. In these last days He speaks to a world that's in the grip of deadly delusions, a world spellbound by the character and activities of antichrist appearing to work in the full panoply of divine power and grace. Satan's final array of deceptions is masterful, compelling, and, for those who remain ensnared, fatal. Jesus warned that Satan's impostures near the close of time would be almost irresistibly convincing. "Take heed that no one deceives you," the Savior admonished, "Many false prophets will rise up, and deceive many. . . . False christs and false prophets will rise, and show great signs and wonders" (Matt. 24:4, 11, 24).

Paul added to the picture: "Let no one deceive you by any means, for that Day will not come unless the falling away comes first, and the man of sin is revealed, the son of perdition, who opposes and exalts himself above all that is called God or that is worshiped, so that he sits as God in the temple of God, showing himself that he is God. . . . The coming of the lawless one is according to the working of Satan, with all power, signs, and lying wonders, and with all unrighteous deception among those who perish, because they did not receive the love of the truth, that they might be saved" (2 Thess. 2:3, 4, 9, 10). Here Paul points out that prior to Christ's coming, a massive *falling away* will occur—a falling away from plain Bible truth on the part of those whose position once seemed solid and unshakable.

Why would this falling away happen? Because the archdeceiver will exhibit amazing signs and wonders, that, to our human senses, will seem more powerful and convincing than Bible truth, especially if our connection with truth and its source is weak. Consequently, "none but those who have fortified the mind with the truths of the Bible will stand through the last great conflict." "Only those who have been diligent students of the Scriptures, and who have received the love of the truth, will be shielded from the powerful delusion that takes the world captive. By the Bible testimony these will detect the deceiver in his disguise." (*The Great Controversy*, 593, 594, 625).

Unveiling Satan's spectacular finale, John the revelator depicted this scene: "Then I saw another beast coming up out of the earth, and he had two horns like a lamb and spoke like a dragon. . . . He performs great signs, so that he even makes fire come down from heaven on the earth in the sight of men. And he deceives those who dwell on the earth by those signs which he was granted to do. . . ." (Rev. 13:11, 13, 14a).

We can see from the language of Scripture that Satan's final counterfeits are not minor deceptions that ensnare only weak, gullible minds. Were it not for their love of Bible truth, and complete faith in it, even God's elect would be deceived by the devil's dazzling signs and wonders that appear holy in character and purpose (Matt. 24:24).

In this supercharged atmosphere of deception and apostasy practiced against the backdrop of diabolic miracles, the Lord sounds a warning. Not in a gentle whisper, but in the rolling thunder-tones of Sinai and Calvary, amplified by the full-scale participation of heaven's angels working in the strength of God for our salvation.

Add to this the corroborating voice of God's last-day Elijah people, and we hear a chorus of impassioned appeal to accept the true gospel in its original power and beauty, divested of all false trappings and all delusive sensationalism. This appeal comes to the world in the form of a telegraphically compressed threefold dispatch contained in Revelation 14:6-12, the message of three angels.

These messages, in combination, present the everlasting gospel. They bear the additional feature of exposing the false gospels of Satan, and hence their seemingly negative quality in certain parts, especially the second and third angels' messages. But these warnings are motivated by all the positive force of God's love. He doesn't want anyone to perish under the influence of deceptions, no matter how thrilling, vibrant, and personally gratifying those deceptions may be.

A young woman who took LSD had such exalted feelings from the drug that she was sure she could fly like an angel. Unfurling her "wings" for a rapturous flight toward mystic realms, she sprang from a rooftop. Her death below moments later brought no joy or salvation into anyone's life. Likewise, many modern notions, held forth as part of the gospel, work to intoxicate unguarded minds with false hopes that clash with plain Bible teachings and lure many into advanced delusions. Examples of these deceptions are the secret rapture, freedom from the moral law, Sunday worship in place of the Bible Sabbath, salvation for those who remain in sin, natural immortality, communication with the dead, "spiritual" or "angelic" messages that purportedly supersede Scripture, and miracles, signs, and wonders posing as Christian while really of demonic origin.

Against this welter of confusion, the Lord sounds His Word, exalting Christ and His righteousness, inviting everyone to freely receive His saving grace that pardons all sin, cleanses the heart, and transforms the human character to joyfully obey the Ten Commandments and exercise loving benevolence, as eternal partakers of Christ's righteousness.

Here is where Elijah's message has its final and fullest proclamation. Let's review the passage we have seen earlier in this book. " 'Remember the Law of Moses, My servant, which I commanded him in Horeb for all Israel, with the statutes and judgments. Behold, I will send you Elijah the prophet before the coming of the great and dreadful day of the Lord. And he will turn the hearts of the fathers to the children, and the hearts of the children to their fathers, lest I come and strike the earth with a curse'" (Mal. 4:4-6).

Note how these last three verses in the Old Testament correspond to the last several verses in the New (see Rev. 22:17-21). Just as Malachi's closing message adjures God's people to obey the law, John's closing message adjures us to heed God's prophecies. In both passages the Spirit of truth emphasizes the Lord's coming and promises to extend a worldwide ministry of reconciliation prior to that event. In both passages the Spirit warns against any attempt to alter or deny God's law or prophetic word, for these are life's unerring guide. To change God's Word in any way is comparable to turning a directional sign the wrong way. Many travelers have been misled by this mischievous device, and in the spiritual sense to change life's signposts is to send people on a road that leads to perdition—not to Paradise. What a serious outcome of accepting error! No wonder heaven's warning against any tampering with the divine Word is so intense, so adamant! But God offers to instill in our hearts a love for the truth that we might be saved.

Differing vitally, however, from the last words of the Old Testament, Revelation closes with warm, vibrant words of invitation and grace. "He who testifies these things says, 'Surely I am coming quickly.' Amen. Even so, come, Lord Jesus! The grace of our Lord Jesus Christ be with you all. Amen." (Rev. 22:20, 21). What a fitting conclusion to the Book of books, whose whole design is to bring people to the Savior and prepare them for His glorious new kingdom, free from the blight of sin and darkness, free to worship Him forever in spirit and in truth. Surely the message of the final Elijah is saturated with this spirit of welcome, joined with an appeal for our steadfast adherence to eternal truth that makes no compromise with falsehood and sin!

Eternal truth permeates the message that God's prophets have borne in every age. But while God brings eternity into view through His prophetic word, He is also keenly aware of time and its unfolding developments. He reveals His major plans to His servants the prophets and gives special emphasis to imminent events that shall vitally affect the world. Hence the concept of *present truth*, truth that is especially applicable to the time in which it is proclaimed but set forth always in a framework of everlasting verities.

An example of this is Noah's message. He preached righteousness and redemption—the everlasting gospel, eternal truth—but he also preached of a coming flood. That aspect of his message was present truth. What if Noah had preached only about God's mercy, love, and forgiveness but had said nothing of His judgment and sentence of doom to a rebellious world? What if Noah had treated the Flood as a mere addendum to his message—a trivial side-issue—or had waited until people asked him why he was building an ark, only to respond with a vague, half-apologetic reference to God's impending judgment? His words would have carried no convincing power, and everyone would have complacently agreed with him that God is good and loving.

But linked with the everlasting gospel of divine mercy, Noah preached about God's retributive judgment coming upon the world. This emphasis alerted people to the unpopular but vitally important truth that humankind is accountable for its sins and that God has fixed a limit beyond which no transgressor can go without incurring divine wrath. Noah preached present truth, thus faithfully warning the world while calling it to repentance. Jesus likened the world of Noah to the world in its final days, a sobering comparison (see Matt. 24:37-39; Luke 17:26-30).

John the Baptist, also a mighty preacher of righteousness, exalted the Lamb of God who takes away the sin of the world. This emphasis logically included the call to repentance. John preached the everlasting gospel as fully as he understood it. Linked with his message was the key element of present truth—the Messiah was in their midst as the God-Man who came to save people from their sins.

It would have been premature for any prophet of former centuries to preach the incarnate presence of the Messiah as a current event. The prophets of the Old Testament preached a Messiah *to come* but not yet manifest. John proclaimed a Messiah who was *here now*, sojourning on earth. This was present truth for John's day and certainly no mere addendum to his message, no optional feature to be taken or left, just as long as one believed in the love and goodness of God and the sacredness of His law, as the Pharisees claimed to do. But because they rejected present truth (and the spirit of eternal truth with it) they crucified the Messiah whose appearance they professed to be awaiting.

Finally, in the extending line of present truth, comes the last Elijah message, with its potent elements of warning and denunciation united with a strong, rich presentation of the gospel. The preaching of Babylon's fall, God's judgment hour, the mark of the beast, and the seal of God and Christ's coming kingdom are no mere addenda to the gospel. Nor are they distracting side issues that obscure the light of Calvary. Rather, the probing searchlight of Calvary, in rays of prophetic light that stream from the cross, illuminate these very issues and show how integral they are to a clear understanding of the gospel.

This understanding includes not only a knowledge of the plan of salvation but also the realization that all sin and error will be swept away in the mighty flood tide of truth bursting forth in heaven-born splendor. Christ's kingdom shall be concretely established after He fully exposes the corruption and moral bankruptcy of every false kingdom, especially Satan's counterfeit "kingdom of God" on earth.

It is good news that God does not let these deceptions multiply and flourish unchecked forever. It is also good news that He does not accept His rightful title of sovereignty until He refutes all of Satan's lying charges against Him. Because Christ is determined that iniquity shall not rise up the second time, He throws every charge open to thorough investigation. Thus His faithfulness and love are fully revealed. When this is accomplished through the investigative judgment, He publishes the decree: "And thou, O deadly wounded wicked one, the prince of Israel [counterfeit Christendom, global Babylon], whose day is come, when iniquity shall have an end, thus says the Lord God: 'I will remove the mitre and take off the crown; nothing shall remain the same [i.e., your absolute power shall cease forever]. Exalt the lowly and abase the exalted. I will overturn, overturn, overturn it. It shall be no longer, until He comes whose right it is, and I will give it Him' " (Ezek. 21:25-27, KJV, ASV, NKJV, combined).

It is good news that the Lord promises the final overthrow of all apostate religion to clear the way for the truth as it is in Jesus to be exalted eternally, without the bellow and bray of rival voices speaking great things and blasphemies in God's name, but not by His authority. It is good news that Satan shall be routed from his nest of power and pride, and Christ shall be eternally enthroned as King of kings and Lord of lords.

And this is the great message of God's final Elijah, the 144,000. The message is a call to make Christ our Redeemer and the Ruler of our hearts, so that we might live for His honor. Let's briefly look at the specifics of God's final appeal to humanity.

*The first angel's message* (Rev. 14:6, 7). This urgent worldwide message is a wake-up call. It is the everlasting gospel whose words are minted in the treasury of heaven's truth and liberally scattered to all the world.

*Fear God and give glory to Him*; that is, return to Him with reverence, honor His authority as supreme, believe and obey His word. "The truth and the glory of God are inseparable; it is impossible for us, with the Bible within our reach, to honor God by erroneous opinions."[2] The call to give glory to God emphasizes obedience to His Word as indispensable to true fellowship with Him. His character shines through those who obey Him, and all true obedience is from the heart, by grace (see Isa. 60:21; Rom. 6:14-17, 22; 2 Thess. 1:10-12). We shall then bring forth fruit for His glory. By revealing His truth and love to others, we shall be instrumental in bringing them to Christ.

*For the hour of His judgment is come.* God has opened the books of record in heaven to reveal the decisions of humanity in response to His mighty labors of redeeming love. Each professed believer's life is now being brought into review, to demonstrate the inner workings of divine truth and grace, thus to prove the effectiveness of heaven's plan to redeem fallen humanity. If the record books reveal a lack of sanctification in our lives, it is because we have not cooperated with God in letting the power of the Atonement do its reconciling, restorative work. We must *receive* the atonement (reconciliation), if it is to save us. Accordingly, our destiny is disclosed in the judgment—a kind of spiritual CAT scan, or inner map of our lives. But that judgment is no sterile, unfeeling process. Christ's intercession continues and intertwines with His work of judgment, which He performs as a betrothal process between Himself and His receptive people.[3] His offered robe of righteousness (wedding garment) constitutes the bestowal of His character on His people, a character that harmonizes with the moral requirements of His law and exhibits His love, purity, and compassion.

Logically connected with the proclamation of God's judgment hour is heaven's call to worship God the Creator. *Worship Him who made heaven and earth, the sea and springs of water.* Because He is Creator and Sustainer, His authority is rightfully supreme. No one can legitimately usurp the prerogatives of the One who gives us life and establishes all the laws of being. To eternally signalize His Creatorship, God instituted the Sabbath as a perpetual reminder that He created us in His image and desires to have growing fellowship with us. Moreover, since the entrance of sin on earth, the Sabbath has taken on the additional significance of being a sign of God's sanctifying grace and power (see Ezek. 20:12). This added dimension fits the function of the Sabbath perfectly because it takes the wisdom and power of the Creator to *re-create* His image in the soul that has been deformed and degraded by sin. That is why the apostle Paul declared, "Therefore, if anyone is in Christ, he is a new creation; old things have passed away; behold, all things have become new" (2 Cor. 5:17).

The very wording of the first angel's message, calling on humanity to worship the Creator, borrows from the fourth commandment. Compare Revelation 14:7 with Exodus 20:11. Naturally this raises the question, "Why does modern Christianity, along with nearly the whole world, reject the seventh-day Sabbath and substitute the first day in its place?" Especially when God commanded us to *remember* the Sabbath day to keep it holy. Prophecy disapprovingly predicts this change, but we will shortly take up this matter in reviewing the third angel's message.

To accentuate the importance of the Sabbath and its commemorative role, God designated its observance as a sign between Himself and His people, a hallmark of their loyalty and love. The Sabbath, therefore, in a special sense, constitutes His seal (see Ezek. 20:12, 20; Isa. 8:16). This application of the term "seal of God" must be understood in the context of the Holy Spirit's character-transforming work for all who obey Him (see 2 Cor. 1:21, 22; Eph. 4:30-32). "The seal of the living God will be placed upon those only who bear a likeness to Christ in character."[4] Thus Sabbath keeping is a seal only to those who are being saved and sanctified by the Lord of the Sabbath, who re-creates us in His image.[5]

Besides pointing to the Sabbath, the call to worship the Creator God directs our attention away from human objects of worship, whether those objects are inventions or inventors of new ideas. We are to worship *only* the Creator. This emphasis found in the first angel's message vibrantly echoes the message and work of Elijah, which was designed to turn the people's hearts away from idol worship to an enlightened worship of the Creator, who governs nature and provides all life's blessings.

Holy angels do not permit anyone to worship them, nor do honest people (Rev. 22:8, 9; Acts 10:25, 26). True worship is not merely homage due from a lesser being to a greater but to the Giver and Sustainer of life. Worship given to any other object or being is spurious and debasing. Once we recognize and appreciate this, we want to understand the character and requirements of our Creator. We honor His authority as supreme, and we rejoice to worship our

God as our best Friend and only Lord. We deem it an honor to serve Him and obey His law by the grace He provides.

The sure knowledge that He has created us in His own image, and that He lovingly provides for all our needs, elevates and transforms our concept of life. We know that we are not our own and are not self-existent. We are not living in a cosmic limbo, void of direction or meaning. We are not emerging from an obscure, undefined past only to drift into an indeterminable, frightening future. For the child of God who believes His Word, life is not an existential journey into the realm of the unknown. God is in control. He knows us and cares about us. While sin has alienated us from our Creator and ravaged our moral nature, He is able, through the plan of salvation, to make us whole again and to reconnect us with Himself in satisfying fellowship (2 Cor. 6:16-18; 1 Thess. 5:23, 24). Knowing God this way gives stability, security, and noble meaning to life.

Had the first angel's message been widely heeded when it first began to be proclaimed in the early 1840s in a purely nonsectarian spirit, it would have brought tremendous revival and reformation to Christendom generally. "The church would again have reached that blessed state of unity, faith, and love which existed in apostolic days, when the believers 'were of one heart and of one soul,' and 'spake the word of God with boldness,' when 'the Lord added to the church daily such as should be saved.' "[6]

The thousands who did accept this message were highly blessed by walking in its power.

> They came from different denominations, and their denominational barriers were hurled to the ground; conflicting creeds were shivered to atoms; the unscriptural hope of a temporal millennium was abandoned, false views of the second advent were corrected, pride and conformity to the world were swept away; wrongs were made right; hearts were united in the sweetest fellowship, and love and joy reigned supreme.[7]

But the Christian churches in general rejected the call to pristine godliness that rings out through the first angel's message. This widespread rejection necessitated the proclamation of *the second angel's message*, *"Babylon is fallen, is fallen, that great city, because she made all nations drink of the wine of the wrath of her fornication."* Christ symbolized His new covenant by a cup filled with unfermented grape juice, typifying the cleansing, life-giving virtue of His blood. Babylon, which is apostate Christendom, dispenses the intoxicating wine of a counterfeit covenant, one that replaces the Word of God with the traditions of men, mingling doctrines of demons with the glorious truths of Scripture, offering up thereby a mixture of confusion, of falsehoods parasitically entwined around sacred verities.

For the third angel's message, read the pointed words of warning and appeal found in Revelation 14:9-12. As you do so, bear in mind that all "His warnings, are but the breathing of unutterable love."[8]

In conjunction with Revelation 13:11-17, the third angel's message shows that church and state will combine forces to become a stupendous dynamo of satanically inspired one-worldism that will allow no dissent. Whoever does not conform to the mark of the beast (compulsory Sunday observance) will become subject to the death penalty. Mighty miracles generated by Satan and his angels will give apparent validity to this program of corrupt unity, and religious intolerance toward all who hold to God's Word above human edicts.

Naturally, those who honor God's commandments must refuse the mark of the beast and stand in vindication of Heaven's unchanging law. These faithful advocates of truth will be visited with special power from heaven to proclaim a faithful warning against receiving the mark of the beast. At the same time, they will urgently appeal to all people everywhere to trust in the true God and obey His precepts through the faith of Jesus. Their strength is not in coerced uniformity of religious practice but in Christ and His righteousness.

Faithfully they repeat God's plea not to suffer the unspeakable agonies of the second death, which Christ alone has thus far experienced in our place. He drank the cup of divine wrath against sin to spare us eternally from this dreadful fate. Having vicariously undergone the anguish of the second death for us, He graphically describes His Calvary woe as a final appeal and warning to desperately deluded men and women, in the hope of alerting them to the fatal folly of casting in their lot with antichrist.

Thus the third angel's message, poignant and impellingly vivid, magnifies Calvary and its purpose. Only by contemplating Calvary can we understand the exceeding sinfulness of sin, the justice of its penalty, the righteousness of God's law, and the fullness of His redeeming grace. Those who keep the commandments of God and have the faith of Jesus persevere under the supernatural power of the Holy Spirit to declare this message of true justification by faith. Although their labors are rewarded by severe persecution leading to a death decree, they are driven on by love for Christ and humanity to continue giving the trumpet of warning a certain sound. The perfect love of God has cast all fear out of their hearts, and they cannot be intimidated. When commanded to desist from their testimony, their answer will be much like that of Peter and John to the Sanhedrin under comparable circumstances, "Whether it is right in the sight of God to listen to you more than to God, you judge. For we cannot but speak the things which we have seen and heard" (Acts 4:19, 20). Constrained by love and the inspiration of the Holy Spirit, they will continue their witness with mounting energy.

> The Lord God of heaven will not send upon the world His judgments for disobedience and transgression until He has sent His watchmen to give the warning. He will not close up the period of probation until the message shall be more distinctly proclaimed. The law of God is to be magnified; its claims must be presented in their true, sacred character, that the people may be brought to decide for or against the truth. Yet the work will be cut short in righteousness. *The message of Christ's righteousness is to sound from one end of the earth to the other to prepare the way of the Lord. This is the glory of God which closes the work of the third angel.*[9]

And so we hear the powerful trumpet tones of the three angels' messages, awakening simultaneous reverberations of Sinai and Calvary and bringing these two mountains into companionship with Mount Zion above, where we see the Lamb and His redeemed flock joyfully assembled. The composite effect of these messages is both hopeful and disturbing. Hopeful because God is near to extend all of heaven's power for our salvation from Satan's force and fury. Disturbing because of the potent, imperative note of warning whose intensity increases through the progress of these messages, like the trumpet blast of God on Sinai that waxed louder and louder until the people's attention was fully turned to the voice of the Lord (Exod. 19:19).

Why the blast-furnace language of warning and command in God's final declaration of the gospel? It is to dislodge people from their complacency and spiritual delirium. Multitudes rejoice in a false hope, believing themselves to be eternally secure while they live in a state of spiritual declension, over which they have applied a glossy veneer of Christianity. Their religion is for them, is far more a cultural affiliation than a spiritual experience. The first angel's message punctures this bubble faith, this glittering illusion, and points to the source of all true spiritual power—Christ, the Creator, who invites us to let Him create in us a clean heart and renew a right spirit within us—who also offers us full protection from the supernatural power of Satan, and full strength to withstand his masterful deceptions and his rage against the remnant, "who keep the commandments of God and have the testimony of Jesus Christ" (Rev. 12:17). The three angels' messages pulsate as a bright beacon of inspired warning against spiritual complacency, indolence, and superficiality.

> This is an age famous for surface work, for easy methods, for boasted holiness aside from the standard of character that God has erected. All short routes, all cutoff tracks, all teaching which fails to exalt the law of God as the standard of religious character, is spurious.[10]

It is to overthrow spurious religion and establish "pure religion and undefiled" that the three angels' messages are given. And before we can meaningfully and convincingly announce these messages ourselves, their power must be the actuating force of our lives. We must be a living exposition of their glory. If not, any attempt for us to proclaim these messages will sound twisted, bitter, and repulsively self-exalting. They are strong medicine, the antidote to all sin and error, and can be properly dispensed only by physicians who are healed by taking that prescription themselves.

After all, who are we to denounce Babylon if we are living Babylonish lives? Who are we to warn against the mark of the beast unless we are receiving the seal of God and all the sanctifying grace that accompanies the sealing? Who are we to call on people to "Fear God and give glory to Him" unless our lives are coming into such resonant harmony with Christ that His character can plainly be seen in our own? These messages are to prepare the way for the second coming of Christ. We need the spiritual power of Elijah, as John the Baptist had, to successfully convey these messages to a spiritually inebriated world. Thus we must walk in the light of God's law and love. For the spirit and power of Elijah are really the spirit and power of Christ. Any spirit deviating from this, while claiming the authority of Elijah, is a travesty and a betrayal of sacred trust.

> The messages from heaven are of a character to arouse opposition. The faithful witnesses for Christ and the truth will reprove sin. Their words will be like a hammer to break the flinty heart, like a fire to consume the dross. There is constant need of earnest, decided messages of warning. God will have men who are true to duty. At the right time He sends His faithful messengers to do a work similar to that of Elijah.[11]

Yet, even so, denunciation of sin and error is not the driving passion of God's last day Elijah people, any more than it was for Elijah the Tishbite or John the Baptist. Their whole aim was to help people become truly reconciled to God and not remain alienated from His fellowship and truth. They carried out the corrective side of their mission with humility and self-abasement. Like Jude, though longing primarily to testify of the joys of salvation, God's last-day reformers are constrained in the Spirit also to "contend earnestly for the faith which was once for all delivered to the saints"

(Jude 3). But those who enjoy blasting away at error and condemning the deceived are not God's choice to bear the Elijah message, even though they may run on a self-appointed mission, full of zeal, but, alas, not according to knowledge. God asks us to be restorers of paths to dwell in, not ravagers of the soul (see Isaiah 58:12).

May we take up this work of restoration in the spirit of Christ's love and sacrificial service.

> At this time a message from God is to be proclaimed, a message illuminating in its influence and saving in its power. His character is to be made known. Into the darkness of the world is to be shed the light of His glory, the light of His goodness, mercy and truth. . . .
>
> *The last rays of merciful light, the last message of mercy to be given to the world, is a revelation of His character of love.* The children of God are to manifest His glory. In their own life and character they are to reveal what the grace of God has done for them.
>
> The light of the Sun of Righteousness is to shine forth in good works—in words of truth and deeds of holiness.[12]

*Questions for Discussion and Reflection*

1. Why is the strong warning component of the three angels' messages compatible with their essential content as the everlasting gospel?

2. How do the three angels' messages give an enlarged picture of God's mercy and justice, without obscuring either attribute?

3. Discuss how the "message of justification by faith is the third angel's message in verity." See *Selected Messages*, 1:372.

4. How have the three angels' messages influenced your religious experience?

1. "Nothing short of obedience can be accepted. Self-surrender is the substance of the teachings of Christ. Often it is presented and enjoined in language that seems authoritative, because there is no other way to save man than to cut away those things which, if entertained, will demoralize the whole being" (*The Desire of Ages*, 523).

2. *The Great Controversy*, 597.

3. Note that at the beginning and at the close of the Day of Atonement [symbolic portrayal of the day of judgment] in the typical service, the morning and evening sacrificial lamb was offered, thereby signifying the continuance of the high priest's intercessory ministry throughout the process of judgment. Moreover, the high priest made atonement for the sins of the people and sprinkled the sacrificial blood of the Lord's goat before the mercy seat seven times, which indicates the fullness and thoroughness of the Messiah's mediatorial work parallel with the work of investigative judgment (see Lev. 16:15, 30; Num. 29:7-11). Consider the betrothal motif in connection with the work of judgment in heaven (Matt. 22:1-13; cf. Hos. 2:19).

4. *Review and Herald*, 21 May 1895.

5. No amount of outward observance will compensate for a lack of inward experience. Likewise, no amount of inward experience will compensate for a lack of outward observance of that which God expressly commands us to do. He has expressly commanded us to keep the seventh-day Sabbath holy, not merely to have a perpetual mystical rest in our hearts, which we then call Sabbath keeping on new covenant terms. True, Christ does give us perpetual spiritual rest from everything that's unholy within (Matt. 11:28-32), but as the Lord of the Sabbath, He commands us to obey His whole law, including the fourth commandment, which specifies Sabbath keeping. The Christian's obedience to the law springs from faith and love (John 14:15). No honest person can call that legalism or old-covenant bondage.

6. *The Great Controversy*, 379.

7. Ibid.

8. *Steps to Christ*, 35.

9. *Testimonies for the Church*, 6:19; emphasis supplied.

10. *Testimonies for the Church*, 5:500.

11. Ibid., 254. See also *Testimonies to Ministers*, 411-415.

12. *Christ's Object Lessons*, 415, 416; emphasis supplied.

# CHAPTER
# 20

# The Spirit of Prophecy

**A**mos had a dual occupation. Living in Tekoa six miles southeast of Jerusalem, he was both a shepherd and grower of sycamore figs. Although a man of deep consecration, it probably never occurred to him that God would someday call him to prophesy. Amos did not attend a school of the prophets and never sought the privilege and burden of being a special messenger (see Amos 7:14, 15). Egotism did not enter into his mission. He had no *personal* hunger to be heard. But when God commanded this shepherd of Tekoa to address the Middle Eastern nations including Israel and her king, Amos wrote, "The Lord God hath spoken! Who can but prophesy?" (Amos 3:8).

This typifies the nature of the true prophetic gift. God's prophets did not seek favor or fortune. Often they dreaded their role, knowing that their straightforward, unflattering messages would isolate them from the people and enrage the rebellious. Moses, Jeremiah, and Jonah were all reluctant to take up their prophetic mission. The work of God's prophets has generally been lonely and thankless. Only because of their love for God and humanity have they persevered in their arduous and dishonored task. Often they were blamed for being harsh, judgmental, doomsaying, malicious, subversive, fanatical, deluded, out-of-touch, reactionary, and antisocial. Many were martyred as society's reward for their faithful labors.

Prophecy that touches on the moral fabric of our lives is feared and hated. But true prophecy is never separable from moral instruction. That, in fact, is its central purpose. It is sent as a guiding light to lead us heavenward in our hearts, to bring us into a close and unstraying walk with Jesus, such as Enoch had. It is this central purpose that gives prophecy its high value and eternal relevance.

God has sent prophets to His people especially at critical junctures in the history of the church and world. He sent Noah before the Flood to warn the world to prepare for its impending judgment. He sent Hosea, Isaiah, Micah, and other prophets before the fall and captivities of His divided nation. He sent John the Baptist before the first advent of Christ, and it is no marvel that He would reinstate the gift of true prophecy just prior to Christ's second appearing. It is a gift of love, of vital communication, sent to help the world prepare for the most conclusive event of all time.

When Christ established His church, He endowed it with the Holy Spirit, that the power of His life and gifts might function through the church for the blessing of the world. The Holy Spirit sanctifies, convicts, instructs, comforts, and communes with believers. It also empowers them as true representatives of Christ and colaborers with Him for the salvation of others and the constant enlargement of His church. It is God's purpose, through the Spirit, to fill us with the fruits of righteousness (Gal. 5:22, 23) and impart spiritual gifts to:

- keep the church united in doctrine and fellowship
- help the church grow spiritually in Christlikeness
- enable the church to minister to the varied needs of the world and thereby add to the family of God
- protect the church from false doctrine and satanic influences
- keep the church awake to its privileges, duties, and perils

See Ephesians 4:8-16 and 1 Cor. 12:1-14. It has been God's purpose since the inception of the church that it should come behind in no gift as it awaits our Lord's return and labors to hasten that day (1 Cor. 1:7). Among the spiritual gifts He has provided His church is the gift of prophecy. Most people equate the gift of prophecy with one function: the ability to foretell the future. But a survey of the lives and work of Bible prophets reveals that their role included far more than prediction of coming events. Their primary function was to exalt the character of God, explain His purposes, uphold sound morals, and keep the spirit of brotherly love glowing in the hearts of God's people. Theirs was an all-encompassing role of guidance. They spoke not on their own authority but as they were moved by the Holy Spirit (2 Pet. 1:21). Christ and His atonement was their overarching and undergirding theme (Luke 24:25-27, 44-48). The ultimate intent of all their predictive work was to magnify Christ and delineate the character of His kingdom and the means of its establishment. (See, for example, Daniel 9; Psalm 22; Isaiah 53; Zechariah 12 through 14.) Their reproofs and warnings of divine judgment were meant to draw God's erring people back onto the path of life, not to inflict shame or discouragement. Reconciliation to God was the keynote of their ministry. They longed to see Christ, the Day-Star, arise in the hearts of people worldwide. Their vision was universal, stretching far beyond the borders of their own time and nation and reaching to the new heavens and new earth.

The gift of prophecy flourished in the early church. Not just the apostles were endowed with this gift; it was widely distributed among believers, both men and women, for the church's edification and spiritual guidance (see Acts 11:27; 13:1-3; 15:32; 19:6, 7; 21:9, 10).

After the first century A.D., however, prophecy substantially ceased to function as a gift in the church. Scripture explains why this gift went into eclipse despite its having been ordained as a permanent part of the church's spiritual constitution. Paul warned Christians in his day that after his departure, grievous wolves would enter the church, not sparing the flock. By speaking perverse things they would alienate some from the general body of believers and draw away disciples after themselves. Paul further predicted a massive falling away from the truth among believers (see Acts 20:28-31; 2 Thess. 2:3-5). And Peter foretold the rise of false prophets in the church (see 2 Pet. 2). But neither Peter nor Paul warned against prophesying. Rather, they said that all prophesying is to be brought to the test of Scripture (1 Cor. 14:31-33; 1 Thess. 5:19-21; 2 Pet. 1:19-21).

In ancient days God warned His people that if they turned their hearts away from His law and testimony, then spiritual darkness would settle over the church and the gift of prophecy would be withdrawn, because it would only be treated as an affront by those who heard the messages of prophetic warning and counsel. "The Law is no more and her [Zion's] prophets find no vision from the Lord." " 'Do not prattle,' " you say to those who prophesy. So they shall not prophesy to you; they shall not return insult for insult. . . . Thus says the Lord concerning the prophets who make my people stray; who chant 'Peace' while they . . . prepare war against him who puts nothing into their mouths. Therefore you shall have night without vision, . . . the sun shall go down on the prophets and the day shall be dark for them" (Lam 2:9; Mic. 2:6; 3:5-7).

Through insubordination to God and rejection of His prophetic messages, the church forfeits the gift. In the centuries following the apostolic era, the great truths of Scripture were distorted or denied by key leaders in many parts of Christendom. Hence the withdrawal of the gift of prophecy.

But Scripture foretells its reinstatement. With the magnificent symbol of a woman clothed in the Sun (Christ's righteousness) and a crown of twelve stars (the wisdom of God's true messengers) on her head, and the moon (God's covenant and word) under her feet, the Lord depicts a remnant people who keep His commandments and have the testimony of Jesus (see Rev. 12:1, 17 and Isa. 61:10; Mal. 4:2; Rev. 1:20; Ps. 89:28, 35-37; Jer 31:31-37; Eph. 2:20-22). The testimony of Jesus is the Spirit of Prophecy, a gift that is bestowed on God's prophets (see Rev. 19:10; 22:9). This gift is restored to the *remnant,* final remaining portion, of the woman's seed for two reasons. First, God restores this gift to a church that is once again committed to keeping His law without adulteration or compromise. Second, prior to His return Christ gives amplified prophetic guidance to His people so that they will be qualified and strengthened for their responsibility to proclaim the gospel to a world as morally degenerate as it was in Noah's day and awash in an unprecedented flood of satanic miracles and doctrines (see Luke 17:26-30; 2 Thess.

2:1-13; 2 Tim. 3:1-5). God compassionately restores the Spirit of Prophecy to counteract deception and magnify Scripture.[1]

It is no wonder that Satan would be inflamed against those who honor Heaven's gifts by seeking to follow and teach the whole counsel of God. "And the dragon [Satan] was enraged with the woman [church], and he went to make war with the rest of her offspring, who keep the commandments of God and have the testimony of Jesus Christ" (Rev. 12:17). But he cannot quench the gift or divide God's people, for the Lord has decreed that, prior to Christ's return, He shall have a movement that is more unified in truth and impregnable to sophistry than the world has ever known (see Eph. 4:8-13; 5:26-32; Rev. 14:1-12). This unity is achieved under the power of the Holy Spirit and through the guidance of spiritual gifts.

To try to obscure the true gift of prophecy and divert people from the true Messiah, Satan will raise up a widely diverse host of false christs and false prophets who will show great signs and wonders so as to lead astray, if possible, the very elect (Matt. 24:24). But because they have elected to follow the truth as it is in Jesus, they are not deceived; they know the voice of the true Shepherd, "and a stranger they will not follow" (John 10:5).

The spawning of ten thousand false christs does not negate the existence of the True. And the proliferation of ten thousand false prophets does not negate the existence of the true gift of prophecy. It does, however, demand that we have a clear, biblically informed ability to discern the true gift. Paul wrote, "Do not quench the Spirit. Do not despise prophecies. Test all things; hold fast to what is good" (1 Thess. 5:19-21).

Let us then look at the basic Bible tests of a prophet.

1. A true prophet's words will be in absolute harmony with God's law and with the whole of Scripture (Isaiah 8:20).

2. A true prophet will unreservedly confess that Jesus is Christ come in the flesh (human nature) to be our Savior from sin (1 John 4:1-6).

3. A true prophet's predictions unerringly come to pass (Deut. 18:22; Jer. 28:9).

4. A true prophet will bear in character and conduct the fruits of holiness (Matt. 7:15-20).

These are the four indispensable tests of a true prophet. False prophets may be rapidly weeded out by applying these tests. Other characteristics of a true prophets are that

- they prophesy in the name of the Lord, not in their own name or anyone else's (Ezek. 6:1-3);
- *God* calls the prophets; they are not self-appointed (Jer. 1:4-9; Amos 7:14, 15);
- they offer no private interpretations of prophecy but are subject to the prophets, in fraternal union with their testimony (1 Cor. 14:32; 2 Pet. 1:21; 3:15-18);
- they point out the sins of God's people and exhort them in the way of righteousness (Isa. 58:1, 2; Ezek. 2:1-10);
- they warn people of God's coming judgment and call people to repentance and faith in the true Redeemer (Zeph. 2:1-3; 3:14-17; Rev. 14:6-12).

Seventh-day Adventists believe that Ellen G. White (1827–1915) had the true gift of prophecy. We believe this because she unequivocally passes all the tests of a true prophet and the fruit of her labors has been abundantly blessed, even decades after her death. She constantly exalted Christ as the God-Man come to be the world's Redeemer; she exalted Scripture; reverenced God's law; accurately predicted events of great magnitude; lived a morally upright life with deep compassion toward all, especially the destitute and afflicted. She was willing to spend and be spent in service to her Lord, and did not seek great things for herself. Even those detractors who personally knew her acknowledged that she was a woman of integrity and compassion. Her non-Adventist neighbors held her in high regard because of her kindly deeds, which included giving food to the hungry, blankets and clothing to the poor, and applying effective home remedies to the sick, free of charge.

Her writings, which are voluminous, all exalt the truth as it is in Jesus and are marked with a high and practical purpose to call people to the standard of righteousness found in God's Word. Further, she gave ample and lucid counsel on how to serve the Lord with solidity of purpose, soundness of method, and grace of manner.

What was Ellen White's perception of her calling and work?

> To claim to be a prophetess is something that I have never done. If others call me by that name, I have no controversy with them. But my work has covered so many lines that I cannot call myself other than a messenger, sent to bear a message from the Lord to His people, and to take up work in any line that He points out.
>
> I have written many books, and they have been given a wide circulation. Of myself I could not have brought out the truth in these books, but the Lord has given me the help of the Holy Spirit. These books giving the instruction that the Lord has given me . . . contain light from heaven, and will bear the test of investigation . . .[2]
>
> Abundant light has been given to our people in these last days. Whether or not my life is spared, my writings will constantly speak, and their work will go forward as long as time shall last. . . .[3]

She succinctly stated the essential purpose of her writings: "The testimonies of the Spirit of God are given to direct men to His Word [i.e., the Bible] which has been neglected."[4] She viewed her writings as a lesser light to direct people to the greater light of Scripture but was unequivocal about the source of her inspiration, which was the Spirit of God. She urged people not to use her writings as a test of faith and fellowship nor as a whip to lash others into submission to divine counsel nor as a bludgeon to censure and condemn those of whom we disapprove. The primary function of her writings, as she saw it, was to stimulate Christians to read the Bible with closer attention and deeper devotion to the practical force of its message.

Consider Ellen White's reverent view of Scripture:

> There is nothing more calculated to strengthen the intellect than the study of the Scriptures. No other book is so potent to elevate the thoughts, to give vigor to the faculties, as the broad, ennobling truths of the Bible. If God's word were studied as it

should be, men would have a breadth of mind, a nobility of character, and a stability of purpose rarely seen in these times.[5]

The fruits of Ellen White's counsel have been in every way favorable, not only to the progress of the church and its mission but also to the welfare of the world at large, which has vitally benefited from the church's active humanitarian service that she promoted by example, pen, and voice.

Through Ellen White's writings the church has been benefited theologically in its appreciation of Christ and His righteousness, which is to be received by faith. She also clarified the great controversy theme that permeates Scripture. Her writings have guided the church into unity of doctrine, not by presenting extra-scriptural concepts but by magnifying the Word and presenting every doctrine in the radiant light of Calvary. She declared,

> The sacrifice of Christ as an atonement for sin is the great truth around which all other truths cluster. In order to be rightly understood and appreciated, every truth in the Word of God, from Genesis to Revelation, must be studied in the light which streams from the cross of Calvary, and in connection with the wondrous central truth of the Saviour's atonement. Those who study the Redeemer's wonderful sacrifice grow in grace and knowledge. . . . Lift up the Man of Calvary higher and still higher; there is power in the exaltation of the cross of Christ.[6]

Drawing inspiration from Calvary's love and directly guided by the Holy Spirit, Ellen White encouraged the church to develop medical and humanitarian work, Christian schools, a Bible-based stewardship program for funding God's work, publishing ministries, religious liberty and temperance work, family guidance, lifestyle standards, counsels on healthful living, godly principles of administration, a clear concept of racial equality, and the call to world evangelism.

It is no wonder that Satan has sought to kindle a hatred toward this guiding light, alleging through misinformed critics that Ellen

White is a cultic figure. Nothing could be further from the truth. Her writings steer clear of every species and grade of fanaticism and self-promotion, exalting rather the pure Word of Scripture and the everlasting gospel of Jesus Christ. The permanent value of her work can never be undermined by misinformed views. For, ultimately, we can do nothing against the truth but only for the truth.

> As the end draws near and the work of giving the last warning to the world extends, it becomes more important for those who accept present truth to have a clear understanding of the nature and influence of the *Testimonies*, which God in His providence has linked with the work of the third angel's message from its very rise.[7]

For a better understanding of Ellen White's work and influence, I recommend Dr. Roger W. Coon's excellent booklet, *A Gift of Light*, available from any Adventist Book Center.[8]

*My personal testimony.* I first became aware of Ellen White's writings in 1973 while living as a hippie in San Francisco. For the previous decade my life had been a conscious but confused search for truth. Psychedelic drugs and mystical religions, whose tales and teachings I pored over, imparted no sustaining peace, no clear guidance. Then through an Adventist dentist and his wife, Frank and Evelyn Earl, I was introduced to the Lord. They provided me with a King James Bible containing H. M. S. Richards's study notes. I became fascinated with Scripture. Long familiarity with the literature of Elizabethan England made the King James Bible easy for me to read from the literary standpoint. But I was often baffled by the concepts presented in the Bible, because I did not yet have the spiritual discernment that results from true conversion. About a year after I became acquainted with the Earls, first as a patient, then as a friend and protégé, they gave me Ellen White's "Conflict of the Ages" series, a five-volume devotional commentary on the Bible from Genesis to Revelation.

Initially I was affected most by the grace of Ellen White's literary style. Accustomed as I was to the qualities of the great classics, I couldn't help recognizing that Ellen White's writing enjoyed a unique superiority over the greatest of secular literary works such as those of Macaulay, Dickens, Conrad, Faulkner, etc. In the entire galaxy of literary stars, not one of the great writers completely escaped producing passages of leaden obscurity and flawed construction. But Ellen White's writings were different. She expressed her ideas with crystal clarity, unmarred by gaudy style, ponderous repetition, or faulty arrangement. She wrote nobly and authoritatively without pontifical conceit. Never did I discover a sentence that was trite, tawdry, or uncouth. Her ideas, while profound and penetrating, flowed with natural ease. Her imagery, though picturesque and vivid, was never tasteless or overwrought. No wasted sentences, no jarring notes, no fanciful notions. *How could anyone write on such a consistently high plane, with such unflagging inspiration?"* I wondered. Without being previously informed, I began to suspect that she was divinely inspired, but I highly doubted that the church that published her writings would have the courage to admit it.

I felt this way for two reasons. First, her works did not flatter human nature and would therefore reprove anything faulty in the church, of whatever denomination. (I did not yet know that the Earls were Seventh-day Adventists.) Second, I knew enough about modern Christianity to sense that any church's claim to have a recent prophet (and a *woman* prophet at that!) would stigmatize it, however unjustly, as a cult. When I found out later that the Adventist Church unabashedly recognizes that Ellen White, as God's messenger, had the gift of prophecy, my respect for the church increased greatly. I knew that this had to be a people of courageous convictions, willing to accept divine counsel and reproof while bearing the world's scorn.

As I gained familiarity with Ellen White's writings, I found far deeper reasons to believe in her inspiration than their sustained literary excellence. I discovered in the pages of her books an extraordinarily deep portrayal of God's character of love and divine mercy perfectly blended with justice. In *The Desire of Ages*, I felt that I was reading a documentary reenactment of Christ's life unmixed with human imaginings. Scripture came to life as under a magnifying glass upon a clearly illuminated background. The more I read these remarkable writings, the more deeply I am struck by their resonant harmony with Scripture. They consistently lead me back to the Bible with heightened appreciation for it and augmented insight. Her writings stimulate me to investigate Scripture with greater depth and interest. True prophets do not wean you from the Bible but weld you to it.

I can only recommend to any reader unfamiliar with Ellen White's writings to drink from this fountain of inspiration and see that it is good.

*Questions for Discussion and Reflection*

1. Identify three reasons why God has given the gift of prophecy.

2. Why does Satan especially hate the divine gift of prophecy?

3. What are four key biblical tests of a true prophet? Why must a prophet pass all four of these tests to be authentic?

4. If you are familiar with them, how have the writings of Ellen White influenced your spiritual experience? If you are not yet familiar with her work, please ask an Adventist friend or pastor for a copy of one of her books, such as *The Desire of Ages, Steps to Christ, Thoughts From the Mount of Blessing, The Great Controversy.* Your request will be gladly granted.

---

1. This is part of God's promised "restoration of all things" (i.e., truths and gifts) that He shall make prior to Jesus' return. See Acts 3:20, 21; cf. 1 Cor. 1:4-9.

2. *Selected Messages*, 1:34, 35.

3. Ibid., 35, 55.

4. Ibid., 46.

5. *Steps to Christ*, p.90.

6. *Sons and Daughters of God*, p. 221.

7. *Testimonies for the Church*, 5:654.

8. To obtain a copy of this book or any of Ellen White's works, call 1-800-765-6955 in the U. S.

# CHAPTER
# 21

# Travail, Triumph, and Translation of God's Final Elijah

**G**od's word is sure, "He will finish the work, and cut it short in righteousness, because the Lord will make a short work upon the earth" (Rom. 9:28). Note the promise is that He will cut His work short in *righteousness*, not in futility, failure, or frustration. This world will be so filled with violence and turmoil in its last days that if Jesus did not cut His work short, no flesh would be saved, but for the elect's sake those days shall be shortened (Matt. 24:22). This does not mean that no people would be *spiritually* saved but that everyone would be *physically* destroyed in the final unleashing of sin's destructive forces, directed especially against the faithful.

It is impossible to give any idea of the experience of the people of God who shall be alive upon the earth when celestial glory and a repetition of the persecutions of the past are blended. They will walk in the light proceeding from the throne of God. By means of the angels there will be constant communication between heaven and earth.[1]

In the closing work of God in the earth, the standard of His law will be again exalted. False religion may prevail, iniquity may abound, the love of many may wax cold, the

176

cross of Calvary may be lost sight of, and darkness, like the pall of death, may spread over the world; the whole force of the popular current may be turned against the truth; plot after plot may be formed to overthrow the people of God; but in the hour of greatest peril the God of Elijah will raise up human instrumentalities to bear a message that will not be silenced. In the populous cities of the land, and in the places where men have gone to the greatest lengths in speaking against the Most High, the voice of stern rebuke will be heard. Boldly will men of God's appointment denounce the union of the church with the world.[2]

As may be expected, the reaction to this message of warning and denunciation will be mixed. Those who have not bowed the knee to Baal but are loyal to God will joyfully heed the warning, whereas the enemies of truth will be stirred to violent opposition. "There is a prospect before us of a continued struggle, at the risk of imprisonment, loss of property, and even of life itself, to defend the law of God."[3]

Like John the Baptist, some of God's faithful messengers will be martyred prior to the close of probation.[4] Their blood will bear a life-giving witness over the earth, to bring forth a more abundant harvest of converts. Other faithful believers, unable to endure the rigors of violent persecution, will be laid to rest prior to the close of earth's probation (Isa. 26:17-21; 57:1). But many of God's final witnesses shall not taste death; they shall be translated, like Enoch and Elijah see (1 Thess. 4:16, 17; Rev. 14:1-5). Whatever the experience of God's faithful people in these closing days, those who participate in God's final work shall be abundantly honored and in heaven will have no retrospective dissatisfaction with the days of their earthly travail (see Rev. 14:13; cf. Rom. 8:18). During the crisis at the close, God's faithful people will be sustained by such Scripture promises as "Fear not, for I am with you; be not dismayed, for I am your God. I will strengthen you, yes I will help you, I will uphold you with My righteous right hand" and "Lo, I am with you always, even to the end of the age" (Isa. 41:10; Matt. 24:20).

Often shall the faithful be claiming these promises, when all appearances are against them and it *seems* that God has forgotten them.

> The season of distress and anguish before us will require a faith that can endure weariness, delay, and hunger—a faith that will not faint, though severely tried. The period of probation is granted to all to prepare for that time. Jacob prevailed because he was persevering and determined. His victory is an evidence of the power of importunate prayer. All who will lay hold of God's promises, and be as earnest and persevering as he was, will succeed as he succeeded. Those who are unwilling to deny self, to agonize before God, to pray long and earnestly for His blessing, will not obtain it. Wrestling with God—how few know what it is! How few have ever had their souls drawn out to God with intensity of desire until every power is on the stretch. When waves of despair which no language can express sweep over the suppliant, how few cling with unyielding faith to the promises of God.[5]

No one will pass through this great time of trouble on the wings of emotionalism or nominal faith. Our connection with God must be real and robust, or we shall discover to our alarm that we are among the five foolish virgins, whose religious experience was a bundle of fatally lax suppositions and vain hopes (Matt. 25:1-13).

Those who pass victoriously through the time of trouble will be doers of the word and not hearers only. They will not have bought into a bankrupt theology acting as a quick panacea to soothe all their anxieties with the offer of unconditional pardon and redemption.[6] They have not settled for slight words of comfort that say "Peace, peace" where there is no peace. Rather, they have determined to experience true religion and undefiled before God, the religion that will stand the test of fiery trial and "brave the world's cold frown." (See Zech. 3:1-8; Mal. 3:1-6; 1 Pet. 4:11-19). Thirsting for purity of heart and holiness of character, they turn to Jesus.

They make Christ their entire sufficiency, not as a substitute for obedience but as the source of their strength to do His commandments and live in harmony with heaven. To them this is not a pious platitude, not a stale legality, but a gripping, glorious, increasingly intense reality. By experience they can declare, "In the day when I cried out, You answered me, and made me bold with strength in my soul. . . . The Lord will perfect that which concerns me; Your mercy, O Lord, endures forever." "Lord, You will establish peace for us, for you have also done all our works in us" (Ps. 138:3, 8; Isa. 26:12).

God's people remain tenaciously loyal to His law, not because they perceive it as the basis of their salvation but because they have the new covenant experience of the law in their hearts, written there by the Savior Himself, who wrote the identical law on tables of stone at Sinai (Ps. 40:8; Heb. 8:10-12). They also have *Christ* in their hearts, who embodies the law in all its moral splendor and manifold features of love.

Having Christ in the heart, the redeemed keep the law with a fullness and sensitivity of response to its finest nuances of application that completely escape the legalist, whose obedience at best is an imitation of fidelity to the law's outward requirements. True obedience to God's commandments is more than a negation of evil; it is an embracing and assimilation of every principle of divine love inwardly known and outwardly lived. Such obedience is imbued with the power of the Holy Spirit. From His throne of infallible judgment, God confirms that this experience is consummated in the lives of the 144,000: "Here is the patience of the saints, here are they which keep the commandments of God and have the faith of Jesus" (Rev. 14:12). For them faith is the substance of things hoped for, not the shadow of things guessed at; it is the evidence of unseen realities, not the vapor of fond dreams.

The integrating and empowering principle of the saints' experience is their assimilation of Calvary love. They have discovered in the cross of Jesus the moral axis of the universe; the hub of grace and glory in full, ever-living display; the fountain of life; the power of salvation; the reservoir of righteousness. Victory in Jesus is the keynote of their testimony and praise. This is why they are able to bear witness for their Lord with such uninhibited vitality and effective influence, even in the midst of the world's concerted opposition. For them the rage of Satan pales before the radiance of God's love, and without trepidation they do exploits in His name, not excusing themselves for lack of talent or time.

Dwight L. Moody tells of a young convert who tried to preach in the open air. Somewhat flustered, he did not preach in well-rounded sentences or with much rhetorical skill. One heartless critic bellowed from the crowd, "Young man, you can't preach, you ought to be ashamed of yourself." "And so I am," he replied, "but I am not ashamed of My Lord, and for Him I'll go on speaking." No doubt the Lord strengthened him for his work and granted him the needed proficiency over time. But in the last days God's people *will* be able to preach—not according to academic rules of fine speech but according to the anointing of the Holy Spirit, which is far better (see *Evangelism*, 699, 700).

> You, O God, sent a plentiful rain, whereby You confirmed Your inheritance, when it was weary. Your congregation dwelt in it; You, O God, provided from Your goodness for the poor. The Lord gave the word; great was the company of those who proclaimed it. . . . Though you lie down among the sheepfolds, yet you will be like the wings of a dove covered with silver, and her feathers with yellow gold.

> And you will be brought before governors and kings for My sake, as a testimony to them and to the Gentiles.

> Therefore settle it in your hearts not to meditate beforehand on what you will answer; for I will give you a mouth and wisdom which all your adversaries will not be able to contradict or resist.

> Then the remnant of Jacob shall be in the midst of many peoples, like dew from the Lord, like showers on the grass, that tarry for no man, nor wait for the sons of men.

> But in all things we commend ourselves as ministers of God: in much patience, in tribulations, in needs, in distresses, in stripes, in imprisonments, in tumults, in labors, in sleeplessness, in fastings; by purity, by knowledge, by long-suffering, by kindness, by the Holy Spirit, by sincere love, by the word of truth, by the power of God, by the

armor of righteousness on the right and on the left (Ps. 68:9-11, 13. Matt. 10:18; Luke 21:13-15; Micah 5:7; 2 Cor. 6:4-7).

The glory of the Lord will shine upon God's people; their witness will not be in vain (see Isa. 60:1-5). Drawing courage from the message, example, and spiritual power of the 144,000, many will joyfully come out of Babylon, when that decision will be supremely perilous from every earthly standpoint, because of the vigilant opposition of those who have rejected truth and chosen the spirit of error.

> I saw those clothed with the armor speak forth the truth with great power. It had effect. Many had been bound; some wives by their husbands, and some children by their parents. The honest who had been prevented from hearing the truth now eagerly laid hold upon it. All fear of their relatives was gone and the truth alone was exalted to them. They had been hungering and thirsting for truth; it was dearer and more precious than life. I asked what had made this great change. The angel answered, "It is the latter rain, the refreshing presence of the Lord, the loud cry of the third angel."[7]

Just as Elijah the Tishbite was to anoint three before his translation, God's final Elijah, the 144,000, are to go forth as Spirit-filled vessels to anoint the world with the light of the three angels' messages. They originate none of the power but are simply clear, open channels for its heaven-sent flow. Seeing his kingdom shaken and doomed, Satan's rage against God's faithful witnesses will boil over like molten lava (see Revelation 12:17; 13:13-18). He will induce his human agents to formulate a death decree against God's Sabbath-keeping people who bear God's seal.

> As the Sabbath has become the special point of controversy throughout Christendom, and religious and secular authorities have combined to enforce the observance of the Sunday, the persistent refusal of a small minority to yield to

the popular demand will make them objects of universal execration. It will be urged that the few who stand in opposition to an institution of the church and a law of the state ought not to be tolerated; that it is better for them to suffer than for whole nations to be thrown into confusion and lawlessness. . . . The argument will appear conclusive; and a decree will finally be issued against those who hallow the Sabbath of the fourth commandment, denouncing them as deserving of the severest punishment and giving the people liberty, after a certain time, to put them to death. Romanism in the Old World and apostate Protestantism in the New will pursue a similar course toward those who honor all the divine precepts.[8]

Just when the united hosts of evil are about to clinch their purpose, God intervenes to effect a glorious rescue. In more than regal splendor Christ leads the hosts of heaven to take His people from the earth and remove them from the grasp of the wicked, who shall be slain by the brightness of His appearing (2 Thess. 1:6-10). "'At that time Michael shall stand up, the great prince who stands watch over the sons of your people; and there shall be a time of trouble, such as never was since there was a nation, even to that time. And at that time your people shall be delivered, every one who is found written in the book"—the Lamb's book of life (Dan. 12:1).

As the time appointed in the decree draws near, the people will conspire to root out the hated sect. It will be determined to strike in one night a decisive blow, which shall utterly silence the voice of dissent and reproof.

The people of God—some in prison cells, some hidden in solitary retreats in the forests and the mountains—still plead for divine protection, while in every quarter companies of armed men, urged on by hosts of evil angels, are preparing for the work of death. It is now, in the hour of utmost extremity, that the God of Israel will interpose for the deliverance of His chosen. Saith the Lord: "Ye shall have a song, as in the night when a holy solemnity is kept; and gladness of heart, as when one goeth . . . to come into the mountain of the Lord, to the mighty One of Israel. And the Lord shall cause His glorious voice to be heard, and shall show the lighting down of His arm, with the indignation of His anger, and with the flame of a devouring fire, with scattering, and tempest, and hailstones:" Isa. 30:29, 30.

With shouts of triumph, jeering, and imprecation, throngs of evil men are about to rush on their prey, when, lo, a dense blackness, deeper than the darkness of the night, falls upon the earth. Then a rainbow, shining with the glory from the throne of God, spans the heavens and seems to encircle each praying company. The angry multitudes are suddenly arrested. Their mocking cries die away. The objects of their murderous rage are forgotten. With fearful forebodings they gaze upon the symbol of God's covenant and long to be shielded from its overpowering brightness.

By the people of God a voice, clear and melodious, is heard, saying, "Look up," and lifting their eyes to the heavens, they behold the bow of promise. . . . They look up steadfastly into heaven and see the glory of God and the Son of man seated upon His throne. In His divine form they discern the marks of His humiliation; and from His lips they hear the request presented before His Father and the holy angels: "I will that they also, whom Thou hast given Me, be with Me where I am." John 17:24. Again a voice, musical and triumphant, is heard, saying: "They come! they come! holy, harmless, and undefiled. They have kept the word of My patience; they shall walk among the angels;' and the pale, quivering lips of those who have held fast their faith utter a shout of victory. . . .

[While the rebellious earth is being engulfed in general destruction, as described in the latter part of Revelation 16 and 18,] graves are opened, and "many of them that sleep in the dust of the earth . . . awake, some to everlasting life, and some to shame and everlasting contempt." Dan. 12:2. All who have died in the faith of the third angel's message come forth from the tomb glorified, to hear God's covenant of peace with those who have kept His law.[9]

The wicked, to their terror and dismay, see and hear supernatural affirmations from heaven that God's law is unalterable and His covenant eternal, while the earth continues its process of tumultuous breakdown. Babylon's forces collapse; Satan's kingdom is overthrown; righteousness and truth stand vindicated. Then Christ resurrects all the righteous who died in past ages. They come forth from their graves in transfigured bodies, fashioned like Christ's own glorious body, perfect, beautiful, immortal, with all blemishes and defects eradicated. "He will swallow up death forever, and the Lord God will wipe away tears from all faces; the rebuke of His people He will take away from all the earth. . . . And it will be said in that day: 'Behold, this is our God; we have waited for Him, and He will save us. This the Lord; we have waited for Him; we will be glad and rejoice in His salvation' " (Isa. 25:8, 9). In the twinkling of an eye, the living righteous, so recently the target of wicked men's homicidal rage, are glorified and begin their ecstatic ascent from this ravaged planet to meet the Lord in the air and join Him in triumphant procession to heaven (see 1 Thess. 4:16, 17; Rev. 19:11-16).

"When the Lord brought back the captivity of Zion, we were like those who dream. Then our mouth was filled with laughter, and our tongue with singing. . . . The Lord has done great things for us, whereof we are glad. . . . Those who sow in tears shall reap in joy. He who continually goes forth weeping, bearing seed for sowing, shall doubtless come again with rejoicing, bringing his sheaves with him" (Ps. 126:1-3, 5, 6).

"So the ransomed of the Lord shall return, and come to Zion with singing, with everlasting joy on their heads. They shall obtain joy and gladness; sorrow and sighing shall flee away" (Isa. 51:11).

What rapturous odes of joy the glorified shall sing we cannot now conceive, nor can we capture but remotely a sense of the boundless ecstasy that will electrify our whole being on the day of ultimate emancipation—the unfamiliar but thrilling delight of glorification, with heightened senses and expanded faculties blossoming into life through the instantaneous power of new creation. "Eye has not seen, nor ear heard, nor have entered into the heart of man the things which God has prepared for those who love Him" (1 Cor. 2:9).

The richest concentration of superlatives we could muster,

the most opulent descriptions we could conjure, fade into nothingness compared to the far more exceeding and eternal weight of glory that constitutes the inheritance of the redeemed. Numberless will be the varied privileges and joys of God's glorified people, but paramount among them all will be the supreme delight and honor of beholding the beauty of the Lord and inquiring in His temple to learn more and yet more of the marvels of His grace (see Ps. 27:4). Jesus prayed that His people might have the ultimate satisfaction of beholding His glory and having God and His love dwelling in them, the same love that flourishes between the Father and the Son (John 17:21-26). All our other joys and satisfactions will be rooted in this experience. Science, art, and nature will not be our gods, but the Creator alone.

"Human language is inadequate to describe the reward of the righteous. It will be known only to those who behold it. No finite mind can comprehend the glory of the Paradise of God."[10]

> As the scene rises before me, I am lost in amazement. Carried away with the surpassing splendor and excellent glory, I lay down the pen, and exclaim, "Oh, what love! what wondrous love!" The most exalted language fails to describe the glory of heaven or the matchless depths of a Saviour's love.[11]

In heaven the saints will be better able to give expression to their thanksgiving, adoration, and joy as they sing the song of Moses, the servant of God, and the song of the Lamb, "Great and marvelous are thy works, Lord God Almighty; just and true are thy ways, thou King of saints. Who shall not fear thee, O Lord, and glorify thy name? for thou only art holy: for all nations shall come and worship before thee; for thy judgments are made manifest" (Rev. 15:3, 4, KJV). Standing on the sea of glass the 144,000 will sing this anthem with full-hearted-ease and supernal harmony, as the voice of many waters in a vast outpouring of irrepressible thanksgiving, adoration, and praise.

But until that day so soon to be, when heaven's arches ring with the melody of celestial joy, let us learn to catch the notes of Zion's song here below. Singing as we go, let us lay aside every weight, and the sin which so easily besets us, and let us run with patience the race that is set before us, LOOKING UNTO JESUS THE AUTHOR AND FINISHER OF OUR FAITH.

*Questions for Discussion and Reflection*

1. What power sustains the 144,000 (God's last Elijah) through the final time of trouble? What is the basis of their faith and hope?

2. Describe what the cross of Jesus means to you today.

3. What blessings do you look forward to most in heaven?

4. Closely examine the song of Moses the servant of God and the song of the Lamb, in Revelation 15:3, 4. Why are the names of Moses and Christ brought together in the title of this song? Ponder this question in the light of Exodus 15; Malachi 4:4-6; and John 5:46, 47. Find how mercy and judgment, law and grace, are sublimely blended in this song and brought together in eternal compatibility.

---

1. *Testimonies for the Church*, 9:16.

2. *Prophets and Kings*, 186, 187. Link this quotation with the following: "As the end approaches, the testimonies of God's servants will become more decided and more powerful" (*Last Day Events*, 201).

3. *Last Day Events*, 150. See also Ps. 119:23, 24, 126, 127, 157-161.

4. But after the close of probation, God will not permit a single martyrdom for His cause. Precious in His sight is the blood of the saints, and He will not permit them to die in vain. Ps. 72:14; 116:15; *The Great Controversy*, 634.

5. *The Great Controversy*, 621.

6. "Many are deceiving their own souls by living an easygoing, accommodating, crossless religion. But Jesus says, 'If any man will come after me, let him deny himself, and take up his cross, and follow me'" (*Signs of the Times*®, 16 June 1890). See also *Selected Messages*, 1:366-368, 377-382.

7. *Early Writings*, 271.

8. *The Great Controversy*, 615, 616.

9. Ibid., 635-637.

10. *The Great Controversy*, 675.

11. *Early Writings*, 289.

# Epilogue

**W**e have come to the end of our study on the message of the three Elijahs. In some minds the question may linger, "Are the messages of Elijah, John the Baptist, and God's final warning message to the world too stern too severe?" God's messages of warning always match the severity of the crisis and the danger. If a man has a button undone, a quiet whisper to inform him will do, but if his house is on fire, he needs to hear a shout of warning.

This world is heading rapidly toward ruin. Most of its inhabitants, oblivious to their danger, fear no divine punishment and think it is impossible to obey God's law. Many believe that His grace absolves them from obedience, that Christ's death purchases unconditional security for all who profess belief in Him, even if they don't conform to His will. In practical effect they perceive grace as an excuse for sin, rather than as the divinely imparted power that enables obedience to God's law.

Elijah's message in the last days is designed to raise up a people in whose hearts the faith of Jesus is supreme and whose lives demonstrate that supremacy by their joyful, devoted, and unswerving obedience to His law, even in the midst of a world crisis requiring all humanity to repudiate that divine law that expressly glorifies God's creatorship, the Sabbath. This final spiritual test is permitted to help the world recognize that humanity has strayed far from a worshipful connection with the Creator and due submission to His authority.

Jesus compared the world's moral condition at the end of time to Noah's day, during which the earth was filled with violence, and human hearts, saturated with iniquity, were absorbed with pleasure-seeking and profit-making (Gen. 6:5; Matt. 24:37-39). His comparison was not overdrawn, for such is the world today, and the prophetic call to repentance, revival, and reformation is widely disregarded. Noah, a preacher of righteousness, warned the rebellious world of the coming Flood. He was treated as a laughingstock, a deluded old man, a source of entertainment for the debauched.

But when the Flood came, Noah's message no longer seemed comical or condemnatory. It did not seem to convey an exaggerated picture of divine justice or wrath. Now his warning words seemed merciful, as they truly were. As the floodwaters rose, earth's lost, guilty inhabitants saw their fatal folly in treating Noah's message as fodder for jesting and a stimulus to defiance.

> Conscience was aroused to know that there is a God who ruleth in the heavens. They called upon Him earnestly, but His ear was not open to their cry. In that terrible hour they saw that the transgression of God's law had caused their ruin. Yet, while through fear of punishment, they acknowledged their sin, they felt no true contrition, no abhorrence of evil. They would have returned to their defiance of Heaven, had the judgment been removed. So when God's judgments shall fall upon the earth before its deluge by fire, the impenitent will know just where and what their sin is—the despising of His holy law. Yet they will have no more true repentance than the old-world sinners.[1]

This passage need not drive any to a grim fatalism that provokes them to say, "Well, if I'm lost, I'm lost, and there's nothing anyone can do about it." That is far from true. Probation is still open for a little while longer. If we heed the call to repentance, we shall be saved, no matter how weak, inefficient, and fearful we may know ourselves to be. His perfect love will cast out all fear and give us the victory, if only we submit to Christ's sovereign love and Lordship in our lives.

> Before the Flood God sent Noah to warn the world, that the people might be led to repentance, and thus escape the threatened destruction. As the time of Christ's second

appearing draws near, the Lord sends His servants with a warning to the world to prepare for that great event. Multitudes have been living in transgression of God's law, and now in mercy He calls them to obey its sacred precepts.[2]

God's call is a call to obedience by grace through faith. And that grace is the gift of God to all who long to possess the purity of character and heavenly love that Christ offers by His gospel. Repent of your sin and spiritual barrenness, receive a new and fruitful life in Christ—this is the essential message of the three Elijahs.

"Seek the Lord while He may be found, call upon Him while He is near. Let the wicked forsake his way, and the unrighteous man his thoughts; let him return to the Lord, and He will have mercy on him; and to our God, for he will abundantly pardon" (Isa. 55:6, 7).

"Or do you despise the riches of His goodness, forbearance and longsuffering; not knowing that the goodness of God leads you to repentance?" (Rom. 2:4).

"We then, as workers together with Him also plead with you not to receive the grace of God in vain. For He says: 'In an acceptable time I have heard you, and in the day of salvation I have helped you.' Behold, now is the accepted time; behold, now is the day of salvation" (2 Cor. 6:1, 2).

May we respond to these earnest appeals and lovingly echo their call, that more of ransomed humanity might be saved before our Savior declares, "It is done!" and returns in blazing glory.

> Watch ye saints, with eyelids waking;
> Lo! the powers of heaven are shaking;
> Keep your lamps all trimmed and burning,
> Ready for your Lord's returning.
> Lo! He comes, lo! Jesus comes;
> Lo! He comes, He comes all glorious!
> Jesus comes to reign victorious,
> Lo! He comes, yes, Jesus comes.
>
> Sinners, come, while Christ is pleading;

## Epilogue

Now for you He's interceding;
Haste, ere grace and time diminished
Shall proclaim the mystery finished.
Lo! He comes, lo! Jesus comes;
Lo! He comes, He comes all glorious!
Jesus comes to reign victorious,
Lo! He comes, yes, Jesus comes.

Phoebe Palmer, 1844

---

[1] *Patriarchs and Prophets*, 100.

[2] Ibid., 102.